Religions Today

Christianity

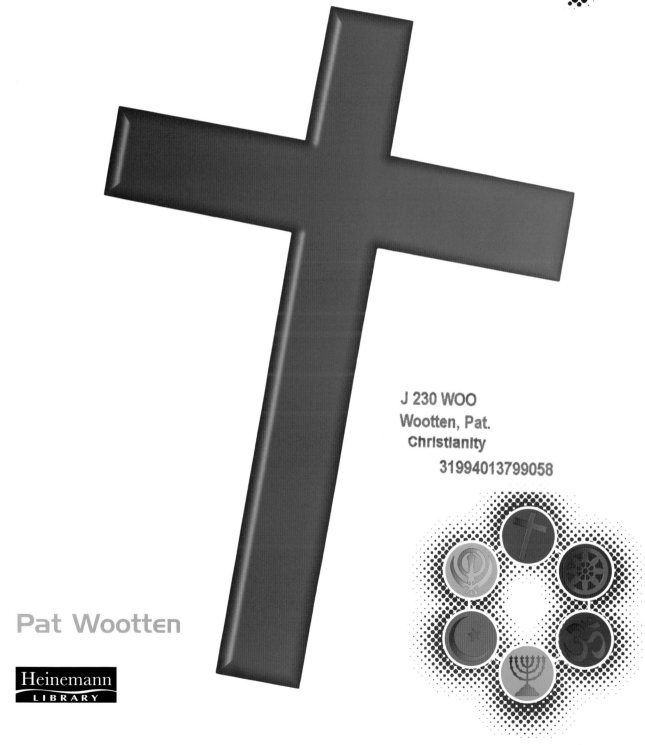

Pat Wootten

Heinemann
LIBRARY

www.heinemann.co.uk/library
Visit our website to find out more
information about **Heinemann
Library** books.

To order:
 Phone 44 (0) 1865 888066
Send a fax to 44 (0) 1865 314091
Visit the Heinemann Bookshop at
www.heinemann.co.uk/library to
browse our catalogue and order online.

Heinemann Library
Halley Court, Jordan Hill, Oxford, OX2 8EJ
a division of Reed Educational and Professional
Publishing Ltd

OXFORD MELBOURNE AUCKLAND
JOHANNESBURG BLANTYRE GABORONE
IBADAN PORTSMOUTH (NH) USA CHICAGO

Heinemann is a registered trademark of Reed
Educational and Professional Publishing Ltd

Text © Pat Wootten, 2002

First published in 2002

ISBN 0 431 14972 0 (hardback)
06 05 04 03 02
10 9 8 7 6 5 4 3 2 1

ISBN 0 431 14979 8 (paperback)
07 06 05 04 03
10 9 8 7 6 5 4 3 2 1

British Library Cataloguing in Publication Data
A catalogue record for this book is available from the
British Library

Typeset by Artistix, Thame, Oxon
Printed and bound in Spain by Edelvive

Acknowledgements
The publishers would like to thank the following for
permission to use photographs:

AKG London/Erich Lessing, p. 14; Andes Press Agency/
Carlos Reyes-Manzo, pp. 10, 11, 18, 24, 25, 26 (right), 30,
34, 36, 44, 46, 51 and 55; The Art Archive/Galleria degli
Uffizi/Dagli Orti, p. 33; Associated Press/Alastair Grant,
pp. 52 and 58 (top); Associated Press/Paras Shah, p. 58
(bottom); Circa Photo Library, pp. 4 (left) and 12; Circa
Photo Library/John Fryer, p. 32; James Davies Travel
Photography, p. 39; Mary Evans Picture Library, pp. 3, 20
and 21; Robert Harding Picture Library, p. 4 (left); Robert
Harding Picture Library/Pearl Bucknall, p. 47; Robert
Harding Picture Library/Jeff Greenberg, p. 54; Robert
Harding Picture Library/David Martyn Hughes, p. 26
(left); Robert Harding Picture Library/ASAP/Garo
Nalbandian, p. 38; Robert Harding Picture Library/Geoff
Renner, p. 40; Robert Harding Picture Library/E Simanor,
p. 40; Impact/John Arthur, p. 35; Panos Pictures/Paul
Smith, p. 42; Science Photo Library/Neil Bromhall, p. 56.

The publishers have made every effort to contact
copyright holders. However, if any material has been
incorrectly acknowledged, the publishers would be
pleased to correct this at the earliest opportunity.

Tel: 01865 888058 www.heinemann.co.uk

Contents

An introduction to Christianity

In this section you will:

● find out how Christianity began and how it spread across the world

● read some interesting facts about Christianity today and what its followers believe.

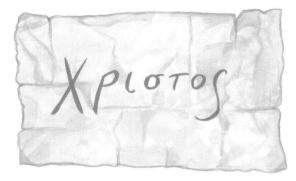

The word Christos, written in ancient Greek

What is Christianity?

Christianity is one of the great world religions. Its followers are called **Christians**.

About two billion people, or one third of all the people in the world, are Christians. There are many different kinds of Christians and they live all over the world.

Christianity began 2000 years ago in Palestine, which is now called Israel.

Map showing the location of Palestine, now known as Israel

The religion is based on the life and teaching of Jesus who was a Jew. His followers, called **disciples**, started a new religion after his death.

Christianity comes from a Greek word 'Christos' which means 'the Anointed One'. This means someone very special sent by God. The **Hebrew** word **Messiah** means the same thing. Jesus' disciples called him the **Christ** when they believed that he had risen from the dead. People began to call the disciples Christians, because they were his followers.

The first Christians wanted everyone to hear the 'good' news' about Jesus. They believed that he was sent by God to be the saviour of the world. The **apostles** travelled to other countries telling people about Jesus. The Romans, who ruled over many countries at that time, did not like the Christians and killed many of them. People who die for what they believe in are called **martyrs**. A young man called Stephen was the first Christian martyr. An angry crowd stoned him to death in Jerusalem.

About 300 years after the death of Jesus, a Roman Emperor called Constantine saw a **cross** in the sky before he went into battle. He won the battle and believed that the God of the Christians had helped him. He became a Christian and made a law which said that Christians must not be harmed. Christianity became the accepted religion of the Roman Empire.

Since the religion began, about 40 million Christians in 220 countries have died for their beliefs. At least 100,000 people were killed because they were Christians in the last 200 years. For example, in modern times, in some communist countries, such as Russia, it was difficult and dangerous to be a Christian. Recent times of change have brought greater tolerance of religious faith.

An artist's impression of Constantine at Milvian bridge before he went into battle

Facts about Christianity

● Christianity began 2000 years ago in Palestine.

● The religion is based on the life and teaching of Jesus, who was a Jew.

● Christianity is one of the world's great religions.

● Its followers are called Christians.

● There are about 1800 million Christians across the world.

● The Christian holy book is called the Bible.

● Christians believe that Jesus rose from the dead after he was crucified.

● Jesus' special friends were called disciples, or apostles.

● The disciples travelled to other countries to tell people about Jesus.

● Some people, called martyrs, were killed for being Christians.

Divisions and denominations

In this section you will:
- find out how **Christians** became divided into different groups
- learn about the main Christian **denominations**.

As Christianity developed, two main groups were in control: the Catholic **Church** based in Rome and the Orthodox Church based in Constantinople, which is now called Istanbul. In 1054, there was a big argument between the head of the Orthodox Church, who is called the Patriarch, and the head of the Roman Catholic Church, who is called the **Pope**. The Patriarch accused the Pope of false beliefs (**heresy**). This was very serious. The two leaders could not agree on what the true beliefs were and so the Christian Church split into two parts. This event is called the **Great Schism**. There were now two main Christian groups in the world.

In the sixteenth century, during a time called the **Reformation**, the **Christian** Church split into more groups. In 1517, a German priest called Martin Luther wrote a list of all the things the Church needed to change. He nailed his list to the door of Wittenburg Cathedral. The Catholic Church in Rome was very angry and Luther was banned from the Catholic Church (excommunicated). Martin Luther and his supporters set up their own Church called the Lutheran Church.

New Churches were set up and four main **Protestant** Churches were formed. These were called Lutheran, Reformed, Baptist and Anglican. The word Protestant comes from the word protest. Over time, other people have become 'fed up' with the

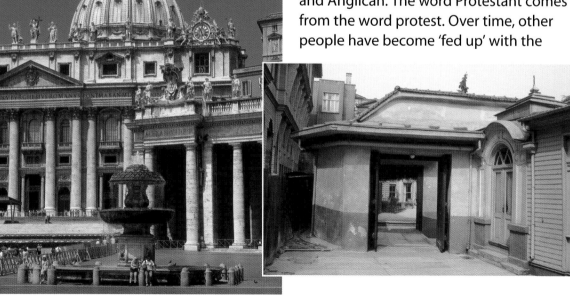

St Peter's Basilica, Rome, and the headquarters of the Orthodox Church in Istanbul

Church they belong to and have broken away to form new Churches. The Methodist, Pentacostalist, Salvation Army and Quaker groups all started because some people were unhappy with their Church and thought there were better ways to be a Christian.

Today there are many different groups within the Christian Church. Each separate group is called a **denomination**. There are about 25,000 Christian denominations. Christians usually belong to a local church which belongs to one of the denominations.

During the seventeenth, eighteenth and nineteenth centuries, **missionaries** travelled to Africa, the Americas, Australia and India to tell people about Jesus Christ. Many people there became Christians.

Christianity is still growing and developing, mainly through the work of the Evangelical Church. Evangelical Christians tell others about Jesus and about what they read in the Bible. In recent years many young people have become Christians through meeting Evangelical Christians.

People who are interested in becoming Christians can attend an Alpha course. Alpha is an evangelical course run by some churches. The course explores the Christian faith through talks and discussions.

Christian denominations today

There are many different groups in the Christian Church. Each separate group is called a denomination. All Christians read the Bible and follow Jesus, but they do not always believe that all the same things are true.

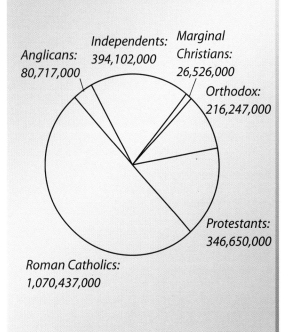

Anglicans: 80,717,000

Independents: 394,102,000

Marginal Christians: 26,526,000

Orthodox: 216,247,000

Protestants: 346,650,000

Roman Catholics: 1,070,437,000

Evidence of Christianity

In this section you will:

● learn what difference Christianity has made to the world

● find out about how Christians describe themselves

● read about the influence of Christianity on education.

What has Christianity got to do with me?

Some people think that religion has nothing to do with them. But religion can still have an effect on our lives even if we are not religious. Look at the diagram below. It shows some of the ways Christianity has had an impact on the Western world.

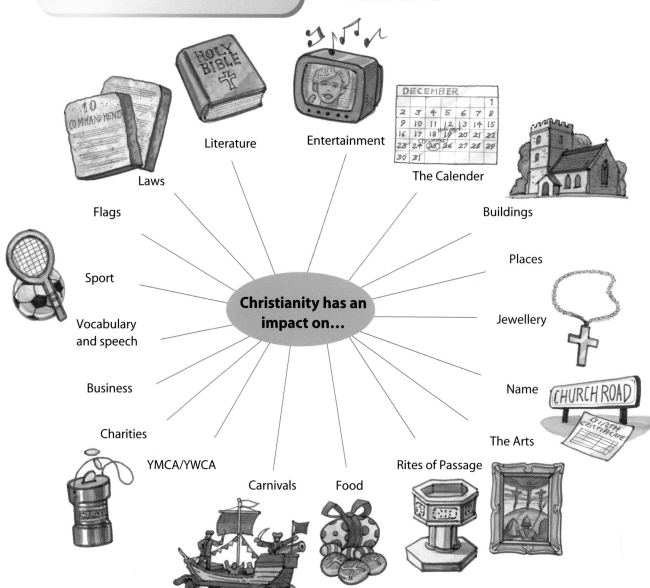

Literature

Entertainment

The Calender

Laws

Flags

Buildings

Sport

Places

Vocabulary and speech

Christianity has an impact on...

Jewellery

Business

Name

Charities

The Arts

YMCA/YWCA

Rites of Passage

Carnivals

Food

Christianity influences many areas of life, including sport, the arts, work and home

What is a Christian?

Christians do not all believe the same things or worship in the same way.

- Some like to pray out loud and listen to a **sermon**, whilst others spend time together in silence believing that they will hear God's voice speaking to them if they really listen.

- Some take part in formal church services whilst others like to clap and sing modern religious songs.

- Some choose to live very simple lives; others make a lot of money.

- Some Christians take part in politics; others think that politics and religion should be kept separate.

- Some Christians agree with divorce; other think that marriage is for life.

- Some Christians think that sometimes war is right; others think that violence and war are never right. These people are called **pacifists**.

The box below shows what some Christians say being a Christian means.

'A Christian is someone who:

… believes in Jesus the Son of God

… tries to live the way Jesus wants them to and loves and helps their neighbours

… belongs to a church and believes that Jesus died to save the world from sin

… believes that Jesus rose from the dead.'

Christianity and education

Traditionally, the ninth Sunday before Easter is Education Sunday. It is a day when the Christian Churches remember Jesus' teaching. Christians also pray for everyone who is involved in education today.

Christianity has made a big difference to education in Britain. Hundreds of years ago, very few children went to school, and not many people could even write their name. Rich children were taught at home by a private tutor, who was often a **priest**.

Some of the earliest schools were set up by the Church. In Victorian times, Sunday schools were established by Christians to teach poor children how to read and write. Dr Barnardo's started as a Sunday school. The Church, or Christian groups such as SPCK (The Society for Promoting Christian Knowledge), also set up many of the great universities.

Today, there are still many Church schools in Britain. Parents often choose to send their children to these schools because they want them to be educated in a Christian environment. Most schools, however, are the responsibility of local education authorities.

Sacred writings – the Bible

In this section you will:

● learn about the Bible

● find out what is in the Bible

● find out what different Christians think about the Bible

● learn about how stories can explain difficult things

● read about different translations of the Bible.

What is the Bible?

The Bible is the **Christian holy** book. The Bible is not one book but is made up of many books. About 40 different people wrote the books at different times over several hundred years. The contents of the Bible are sometimes called **scriptures**. The word Bible comes from the Greek word 'biblia', which means 'books'.

What does the Bible contain?

The Bible is divided into two parts – the **Old Testament** and the **New Testament**.

The Old Testament was first written in **Hebrew** which is the ancient language of the Jews. It is also the Jewish holy book. The Jews call it the **Tenakh**. Jesus was a Jew and would have read and listened to the Old Testament.

Most Bibles have 39 books in the Old Testament. Some books tell stories of the history of the Jewish people. Others are

The Old Testament		The New Testament		The Apocrypha
Genesis	Ecclesiastes	Matthew	1 Timothy	1 Esdras
Exodus	Song of Songs	Mark	2 Timothy	2 Esdras
Leviticus	Isaiah	Luke	Titus	Tobit
Numbers	Jeremiah	John	Philemon	Judith
Deuteronomy	Lamentations	Acts	Hebrews	Esther
Joshua	Ezekiel	Romans	James	The Wisdom of Solomon
Judges	Daniel	1 Corinthians	1 Peter	Sirach (Ecclesiasticus)
Ruth	Hosea	2 Corinthians	2 Peter	Baruch
1 Samuel	Joel	Galatians	1 John	The Letter of Jeremiah
2 Samuel	Amos	Ephesians	2 John	The Song of the Three
1 Kings	Obadiah	Philippians	3 John	Young Men
2 Kings	Jonah	Colossians	Jude	Susanna
1 Chronicles	Micah	1 Thessalonians	Revelation	Bel and the Dragon
2 Chronicles	Nahum	2 Thessalonians		The prayer of Manasses
Ezra	Habakkuk			1 Maccabees
Nehemiah	Zephaniah			2 Maccabees
Esther	Haggai			
Job	Zechariah			
Psalms	Malachi			
Proverbs				

How the Christian Bible is made up

books of rules, stories, songs, poems and prophecy. Prophecy tells about what will happen in the future. The Roman Catholic Bible includes another collection of books called the **Apocrypha**.

Christians believe that the Old Testament tells us about Jesus coming as the saviour of the world (the **Messiah**). They believe this is told by the **prophets** who were holy men who could see into the future. Jesus (the Messiah) would be sent by God to bring peace to the world. Christians believe that Jesus is the Messiah. The Jews believe that God has not sent the Messiah yet.

The New Testament was first written in Greek. There are 27 books in this part of the Bible. The first four of the books are called **Gospels**, which means 'good news'. Christians believe that Jesus was sent by God, which was 'good news' for the world.

The Gospels tell us mostly about the last few years of Jesus' life and especially about the last week of his life which is called **Holy Week**. The New Testament also tells us about how the Christian **Church** began after the death of Jesus and what Christians at that time thought the future of Christianity would be.

Christian attitudes towards the Bible

All Christians believe that the Bible is very important. They believe that it tells them about God and what God wants for them. Some Christians, called fundamentalists, believe that the words in the Bible are what God actually said – word for word. They believe that everything in the Bible is true because God doesn't make mistakes.

Other Christians believe that the writers have written in their own words what God said but that the Bible is still true. Another group of Christians believes that the writers have used stories and symbols to explain what they think God meant. They do not think that everything in the Bible is completely true because the writers may not have understood what God wanted them to write.

Translations of the Bible

- The Bible was first written in Greek and Hebrew.

- In the fourth century CE, St Jerome translated the Bible into Latin. This version is called the Vulgate and was used by the Roman Catholic Church for 1000 years.

- In 1495, a priest called John Wycliffe translated the Vulgate Bible from Latin into English. The Church did not think that ordinary people should read the Bible, and they burnt Wycliffe's work.

- In 1525 CE, another priest, called William Tyndale, began translating the Bible into English from the original Greek and Hebrew writings.

- In 1611 CE, King James asked scholars to make William Tyndale's translation 'even better'.

How Christians use the Bible

In this section you will:

● find out how Christians use the Bible

● learn about what the Bible means to Christians today.

How do Christians use the Bible?

Christians believe that God 'speaks to them' through the Bible. They might read the Bible when they have a problem and need help or comfort because they are upset.

Some Christians read the Bible every day as part of their private devotion. They may use a **lectionary** which tells them what to read each day. Sometimes groups of Christians will meet together to read and discuss the Bible. Parts of the Bible are read out in **church** services. Christians believe that reading the Bible regularly helps them to understand how God wants them to live.

It is important for many Christians that they tell others about their faith. One way they do this is to give away magazines and books about Jesus. Sometimes they leave them where other people may pick them up and read them.

Gideons International is a Christian organization which puts Bibles in places such as hotel bedrooms, prisons and doctors' waiting rooms. They also give away copies of The **New Testament** to pupils in schools. Many people have become Christians by reading about Jesus in this way.

The Bible is an all-time best-seller. More copies are sold every year than any other book. Some parts of the Bible have been translated into more than 2200 different languages. The Bible is also on CD-ROM, cassette and the Internet. It is printed in Braille for blind readers. The United Bible Society translates and produces parts of the Bible to send all over the world. They want to provide **scriptures** in languages that people can understand and at a price they can afford.

The Bible is a source of inspiration, comfort and guidance for most Christians

What do Christians say about the Bible?

'I read the Bible whenever I have a problem or need help.'

'I really enjoy studying the Bible – there is always something new to learn.'

'I believe that God speaks to us through the Bible, so we know what he expects of us.'

'The Bible is the most amazing book… full of stories and helpful advice.'

'The Bible tells me about Jesus… it makes him real.'

'Reading the Bible makes me feel closer to God.'

'I believe that by showing respect for the Bible, I am showing respect to God.'

Mary Jones' Bible

Mary Jones was born in Wales in 1784 CE. Mary could read and write, and she loved to read the Bible – but her family were too poor to own one. Mary wanted to buy her own Bible. She worked hard for six years, doing all kinds of jobs to earn a few pennies. At last, she had enough money but there was nowhere to buy a Bible in her village.

Mary walked 25 miles to the town of Bala. When she finally got there, there was only one Bible for sale, and that was being kept for someone else. The Reverend Thomas Charles listened to Mary's story and gave her the Bible. He decided that the other person could wait a little longer for their copy! Mary's story led to the founding of the British and Foreign Bible Society.

Jesus

Who is Jesus?

Jesus is the most important figure in Christianity. The **Gospels** tell us about Jesus' life and his teachings, his **ministry** his death and **resurrection**. The **Christian** faith is based on this information.

What did Jesus look like?

Christians all over the world have produced images of Jesus although no one knows exactly what he looked like

Curriculum Vitae for Jesus

Names given to Jesus by his followers: Jesus **Christ**, Son of God, the **Messiah**, **Saviour**, Son of Man, Lord.

Names given to Jesus by his enemies: King of the Jews, Blasphemer, Rebel.

Date of birth: Not known exactly but about 2000 years ago. 25 December is celebrated as his birthday.

Place of birth: Bethlehem, Palestine (now called Israel).

Home town: Nazareth, Palestine (now called Israel).

Parents: Mary, God and Joseph.

Religion: Jewish.

Occupation: Carpenter and rabbi (a Jewish teacher).

Hobbies and interests: Healing and helping others, storytelling, teaching people about God, working miracles, being with his friends.

Closest friends: Lazarus, Mary and Martha, Mary Magdalene and the twelve **disciples**: Simon Peter, John, James, Matthew, Bartholomew, Andrew, Judas Iscariot, Thomas, James, Judas, Simon and Phillip.

Other people he cared about: The poor, the sick, anyone in trouble or need.

Important events in his life:

- taken to the temple as a baby

- taken to Egypt to escape Herod's soldiers

- lost on a visit to Jerusalem and found three days later in the temple

- baptized in the River Jordan by his cousin John the Baptist before he started his ministry

- performed his first miracle: turning water into wine at a wedding

- rode into Jerusalem on a donkey on **Palm Sunday** at the start of **Holy Week**

- overturned the traders' tables in the temple

- shared a '**Last Supper**' with his disciples, and told them to eat bread and drink wine in memory of him

- stood trial and was sentenced to death by the Roman Governor, Pontius Pilate

- death by crucifixion

- overcame death on **Easter Sunday**

- went back to heaven to be with God (the **Ascension**).

Special achievements:

- spent 40 days and nights in the desert and did not give in to the devil

- healed the sick and disabled

- raised Lazarus from the dead

- fed 5000 people with two loaves and five fishes

- walked on water and calmed a storm

- overcame death (the **Resurrection**)

- saved the world from sin (**redemption**)

- helped people to know God better (**reconciliation**).

Where do Christians believe Jesus is today?

Christians believe that Jesus is 'alive'. They cannot see him because he is in Heaven with God, but his **Holy Spirit** is at work in the world. Some Christians say they have met Jesus or felt him near them. They say that this was a wonderful experience which changed their lives. We call this a religious experience. Religious experiences can take many forms, but when they happen people believe that they have come very close to God.

A 'meeting' with Jesus

Anthony Bloom is the leader of the Russian Orthodox Church in Britain. When he was a teenager, he was unsure about Christianity. One day, he was reading the Bible, when he suddenly felt that there was someone standing opposite him on the other side of his desk. This is what he said:

'… the certainty was so strong that it was Christ standing there that it has never left me. This was the real turning point. Because Christ was alive and I had been in his presence, I could say with certainty that what the Gospel said about the crucifixion was true.'

The early Christian leaders

Peter

Peter was one of Jesus' twelve **disciples**. Jesus changed his name from Simon to Peter. The name Peter comes from the Greek word 'petros', which means rock. Jesus told Peter that he would be the 'rock'

An early Christian sculpture showing Jesus (centre) with the apostles Peter and Paul

on which he would build his **Church**.

> And so I tell you Peter: you are a rock, and on this rock foundation I will build my Church, and not even death will be able to overcome it.
>
> Matthew 16: 18

After Jesus' death, Peter became the leader of the first **Christians**. He travelled to many countries to tell people about Jesus. In the **New Testament**, we can read letters (**epistles**), which he wrote to two of the churches he set up. Peter was often in great danger. He was put in prison and, in the end, he was killed for his beliefs. He was crucified in Rome in about 67 CE.

Peter was one of the Christian **saints**. He became the first **Pope** of the Roman Catholic Church. St Peter's Basilica in Rome was built in his honour and his remains were placed there in a **shrine**. Millions of Christians visit the shrine every year. Peter is often shown standing next to Jesus in paintings and in stained-glass windows.

Christians like to read about Peter. He did not always get things right. He made mistakes, but he was still chosen by Jesus to look after and lead his followers. Before Jesus was crucified, Peter denied that he knew Jesus three times.

Paul

The New Testament also tells us about another important early Christian, called Paul. Paul is sometimes called an **apostle**, although he was not one of the twelve disciples. Many people think that Paul told more people about Jesus than anyone else and that he made Christianity into a worldwide religion.

Paul was not always a Christian, neither was he always called Paul. He was a Jewish Roman citizen called Saul who hated the Christians and made their lives a misery. Some people think that Paul was responsible for the death of Stephen, the first Christian to die for his beliefs (**martyr**).

Then something happened to change his life forever. Paul was on a journey from Jerusalem to Damascus to arrest more Christians, when a bright light from the sky made him fall to the ground. He heard a voice saying, 'Saul, Saul! why do you persecute me?' Saul was terrified and asked, 'Who are you, Lord?' 'I am Jesus, whom you are persecuting', the voice said. 'But get up and go into the city and you will be told what to do.'

The men who were with Saul also heard the voice but saw nothing. Saul got up and opened his eyes but he could not see, he was blind. His friends took him by the hand and led him into Damascus. Saul did not eat or drink for three days. Then a Christian called Ananias visited him and cured his blindness.

Saul was sure that Jesus had spoken to him. He became a Christian and changed his name to Paul. He went off into the desert for several years so that he could think and pray about what he should do with his life. Later he became the greatest missionary in the history of the Christian Church. He believed that the 'good news' of Jesus was for everyone, both Jews and Gentiles (non-Jews). He travelled around the Roman Empire preaching about Jesus and setting up new Churches. In the New Testament we can read the epistles, which he wrote to these churches. No one really knows what happened to Paul but many believe he was killed by the Roman Emperor Nero in 64 CE.

Paul is also a Christian saint and is often shown standing close to Jesus in Christian art.

Paul's missionary journeys

Paul made four separate missionary journeys around the Roman Empire, and set up many churches.

- *First journey*. In 45 or 46 CE, from Antioch in Syria to Cyprus and Turkey.

- *Second journey*: In 48–51 CE, from Antioch, to revisit the churches he had set up on his first journey; then on to Greece to stay in Corinth for 18 months.

- *Third journey*: About 53 CE, from Antioch to Ephesus in Turkey, then on to Greece before going back to Turkey and then by ship to Jerusalem.

- *Fourth and last journey*: This journey was different. Paul was arrested in Jerusalem and taken to Rome via Malta because of a shipwreck. No one really knows what happened after the trial, but many believe that the Roman Emperor Nero executed him.

Leaders of the Christian Church

In this section you will:

● find out how the three main Christian Churches are organized

● find out what a priest does

● learn about the **Pope** and what Roman Catholics believe about him.

Today, most **Christians** belong to one of three main **denominations**. They are either Protestant, Orthodox or Roman Catholic. These denominations all have people who are responsible for organizing and taking care of things. They all have senior **priests** called bishops who lead and look after all the other priests.

The table below shows how the three main **Churches** are organized.

Name of Church	The Protestant Churches	The Roman Catholic Church	The Orthodox Churches
Divisions within the Church	The Protestant Churches include all the denominations that started after the **Reformation**. In England, the main denomination is the Church of England.	There is only one Roman Catholic Church.	The Orthodox Church is made up of fifteen national or regional Churches.
Leaders and followers	Members of the Church of England are called Anglicans. Each protestant denomination is organized differently. Some involve ordinary people from the **congregation** (**laity**). The Queen is the head of the Church of England. Two Archbishops (senior bishops) run things for her and they are helped by bishops who look after a diocese made up of lots of churches. Archdeacons help the bishops do their work and the priests and vicars look after specific churches and communities. Priests are often helped by deacons, who are training to be priests.	Members of the Roman Catholic Church are called Roman Catholics. There is one leader called the **Pope**. The Pope is elected by cardinals. Under the cardinals are the bishops who are responsible for a diocese, which is made up of lots of churches. Priests look after specific churches and communities and are helped by deacons who are training to be priests.	Members of the Orthodox church are called Orthodox Christians. Each of the fifteen Orthodox Churches is independent. The leader is called a Patriarch which means 'great father'. Under each Patriarch are bishops who are responsible for a diocese, which is made up of lots of churches. Priests look after specific churches and communities and are helped by deacons – people who are training to be priests.
Women priests	The Church of England has had women priests since 1994.	There are no women priests.	There are no women priests.
Religious orders	The three main denominations each have monks and nuns, groups of men and women who take special vows and dedicate their lives to serving God. Some live and work in the community but many have little contact with the outside world and spend most of their time studying, going to church services and praying.		

What does a priest do?

One of the main jobs of a priest is to look after the spiritual welfare of people in their parish. This means they are responsible for teaching them about God and helping them to live as Christians. Priests can forgive people in the name of God. They can take services, including **Holy Communion**, when Christians eat bread and drink wine which has been blessed in memory of Jesus. They can baptize people and carry out wedding ceremonies and funeral services.

Priests also try to visit and look after the sick, lonely or depressed. They also visit people in prison. Some priests might run youth groups or clubs, visit schools or take part in other church events. They have to go to many meetings. Priests must also find time to read the Bible, reflect and to pray.

The role of the Pope

- The role of the Pope is based on Peter, the disciple who Jesus chose to lead and look after Jesus' followers.
- The Pope is the leader of the Roman Catholic Church.
- He is elected to be Pope for life by cardinals, who are the most senior priests.
- He lives in the Vatican in Rome.
- Roman Catholics believe that the Pope is God's representative on Earth, and that God makes him infallible, which means that he cannot make mistakes.
- They believe that the Pope has authority from God to lead the church, to forgive sins and to discipline members who do not follow the Church's teaching.

'A day in the life of an Anglican priest'

9.00am–9.30am Morning prayer service.

9.30am–10.00am Personal prayers and reflection.

10.00am–11.00am Mid-week Holy Communion service.

11.00am–11.30am Coffee with church youth worker.

11.30am–1.00pm Hospital visits.

2.00pm–3.30pm School assembly and meeting with teachers.

4.00pm–5.00pm Home visit to comfort family of someone who has died and help plan the funeral.

6.30pm–7.30pm **Confirmation** class.

8.00pm–8.30pm Paperwork and getting ready for the next day.

8.30pm–9.00pm Reading through meeting agenda and notes.

9.00pm–9.30pm Personal reflection and prayers.

What do Christians believe?

In this section you will:

● study the Apostles' Creed which says what Christians believe

● find out what Christians believe to be true about God, Jesus, the world and life after death

● learn about the Nicene Creed and read some of its words.

Infant baptism is the ceremony by which babies and children are welcomed into the Christian Church

When Christianity began there were lots of arguments about what different groups of **Christians** believed to be true. Christian leaders thought that it was important that everyone knew and agreed about the basics of the Christian faith. In the fourth century CE, two statements of belief called **creeds** were written. The word creed comes from the Latin word 'credo' which means 'I believe'. The **Apostles'** Creed is a summary of the teachings of the twelve **disciples** and sets out the main Christian beliefs.

The Apostles' Creed is **ecumenical**. This means that most Christians accept what it says. The Anglican and Roman Catholic Churches use the Apostles' Creed during daily prayer and worship. The creed is also used during the **baptism** service because it describes the faith into which the baby is being baptized.

The Apostles' Creed

I believe in God, the Father almighty,
Creator of heaven and earth.
I believe in Jesus **Christ**, God's only Son,
our Lord.
He was conceived by the **Holy Spirit**
And born of the **Virgin Mary**.
He suffered under Pontius Pilate,
Was crucified, died and was buried.
He descended to the dead.
On the third day he rose again.
He ascended into heaven,
And is seated at the right hand of the Father.
He will come again to judge the living and the dead.
I believe in the Holy Spirit,
The holy catholic church,
The communion of saints,
The forgiveness of sins,
The **resurrection** of the body,
And the life everlasting. Amen.

What does the Apostles' Creed tell us about Christian beliefs?

It tells us that Christians believe that:

● there is only one God

- God has shown himself to the world in three ways: as God the Father, God the Son and God the Holy Spirit

- the three 'persons', or 'parts', in one God are called the **Trinity**. The word 'trinity' comes from 'tri-unity', meaning three in one

- each 'person', or 'part', of the Trinity has a special function: God as the Father created Heaven and Earth. God as the Son is the saviour of the world. God as the Holy Spirit is the invisible power which helps, guides and inspires people. Christians agree that the Trinity is mysterious and very difficult to explain.

- Jesus is the Son of God, sent to earth to save the world from **sin**

- Jesus' death on the cross made up for everything that humans had done wrong since God created them

- Jesus made it possible for people to really 'know' what God is like

- Jesus was human but also God. This mystery is called the **Incarnation**

- Jesus died on a cross and was put in a tomb but three days later he rose from the dead. This is a very important part of Christian belief called the Resurrection

- Jesus went back to be with God in Heaven and 'sits at his right hand'

- Jesus will come back to earth one day to judge people and decide who will go to Heaven. This is called the **Second Coming**.

Christians also believe that:

- there is life after death, that is, when they die they go to be with God. This is very important to Christians. Christians who have already died are now with God. This is called **eternal life**

- God forgives people when they are truly sorry for things they have done wrong. **Forgiveness** and **repentance** are important themes in Christianity.

The Nicene Creed

The Nicene Creed sets out what most Christians believe. It states that:

- there is only one God who created all things

- Jesus is God's son

- he was born to the Virgin Mary through the power of the Holy Spirit

- he died and rose again from the dead

- he now lives with God.

These are some statements from the creed.

'We believe in one God,
the Father, the Almighty,
maker of heaven and earth,
of all that is seen and unseen…
We believe in one Lord, Jesus Christ,
the only Son of God…
… through him all things were made…
He came down from heaven…'

Sources of Christian belief

In this section you will:

● find out about why Christians believe what they believe

● learn about how some Christian think they have 'seen' or 'heard' God

● read about Cliff Richard and the importance to him of his faith.

Christians believe that God makes Himself known to human beings. Christians call this experience **revelation**.

Christians believe that Jesus, through his life, death and **resurrection** (when he rose from the dead), showed us what God is like. God showed us through Jesus how He wanted us to live.

We also know a lot about God from the Bible. Many Christians believe that God 'speaks' to them through the words in the Bible.

World-class athlete Jonathan Edwards claims:

'The Bible is God's words to me, to all of us, to what my attitudes, my actions and the way I live my life should be. From the Bible I take the basic philosophy of what I try to do – to glorify God through every aspect of my life.'

Many Christians believe that the **Holy Spirit** 'speaks' to them. Some feel so full of happiness and love for God that they clap or raise their hands in the air when they sing hymns and religious songs. Some Christians say that the Holy Spirit helps them to express how they feel in dance or by speaking in a special prayer language called 'tongues'.

Many Christians claim to have seen or heard God in a dream or in a vision. They believe that these experiences have helped them to understand what God is like and how God wants them to live their lives.

Julian of Norwich

Julian of Norwich lived hundreds of years ago in the Middle Ages. She was a nun who lived on her own and spent all her time thinking about God and praying. Once, when she was so ill she thought she was dying, she had sixteen visions in which God showed her how much he loved her. She did not die but lived on and wrote two books about her experiences. She surprised everyone by talking and

Julian of Norwich lived in a cell, or small room, adjoining a church

writing about God as 'Mother'. In those days, most Christians thought of God as 'Father', as many do today.

Julian was well known for being optimistic (always being upbeat) when life was difficult. She used to say 'All shall be well and all shall be well, and all manner of things shall be well.'

St Francis of Assisi

Francis of Assisi was born in Italy during the twelfth century. He claimed to have had several personal experiences with God, which changed his life.

One day when he was out riding he met a leper. The disease made the man look hideous but Francis felt full of pity and kissed the man's hand. The leper kissed

him back and Francis, instead of feeling disgusted, felt full of joy. A few moments later the leper had vanished! Francis believed that he had been tested by God and passed the test. A little while later Francis was praying in a run-down old church, when he heard a voice coming from the crucifix telling him to 'repair my church'. Francis not only repaired the church but also became the leader of a religious order, a community of monks who lived the way the Bible tells us Jesus lived.

St Francis is often pictured with animals, with whom he had a special relationship

Cliff Richard

Sir Cliff Richard has been famous as a singer for more than 40 years. He is a Christian, and believes that God speaks to him through the Bible and guides him about how to live his life. He always appears very upbeat in public interviews, and some of his songs have religious themes. At Christmas in the year 2000, he made a 'pop version' of the Lord's Prayer, which made it to the top of the charts.

Some people have teased Sir Cliff about his religious beliefs, but he still speaks openly about his Christian faith. He has thousands of loyal fans who admire and enjoy his singing and respect the way he lives his life.

Symbols of the Christian faith

In this section you will:

● learn about some of the most important Christian symbols and what they tell us about what Christians believe

● find out what these symbols mean to Christians today.

The cross and crucifix

The **cross** is the main symbol of Christianity. Some **Christians** see the cross as a reminder of Jesus' sacrifice by dying on the cross. Others see the cross as a sign of **salvation** (being saved from sin) or as a sign of humans coming closer to God. This is because when Jesus died on the cross all sins were forgiven. Most Christians agree that the cross is a symbol of their belief in life after death because Jesus rose from the dead.

The cross is used as a sign as well as a symbol. On maps, a cross marks where you will find a church.

The **crucifix** is a special kind of cross. It shows an image of Jesus being crucified.

This symbol focuses on the death and suffering of Jesus.

Bread and wine

Bread and red wine are used as symbols for Jesus' body and blood. The **Gospels** say that before Jesus died, he shared a special meal with his **disciples**. This is known as the **Last Supper**. He asked the disciples to eat bread and drink wine in memory of him. Today this is an important part of Christian worship.

Then Jesus took a cup… and said, 'Take this and share it amongst yourselves…' Then he took a piece of bread… broke it, and gave it to them, saying, 'This is my body which is given for you. Do this in memory of me.'

Luke 22: 17–19

Water

Many people see water as a symbol of life.

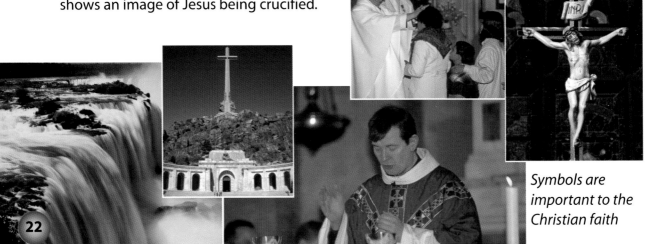

Symbols are important to the Christian faith

Every living thing needs water. Christians use water as a symbol of new life with God.

Oil

Some Christians use oil as a symbol of healing. Sometimes Christians who are sick are **anointed** with **consecrated** oil (oil that has been blessed) in the hope that God will make them better. Sometimes oil is used during **confirmation**, when people make their own promises to be Christians and become full members of the **Church**. The Orthodox Church uses oil in the service of **chrismation**, which follows the **baptism** service. This shows that all wrong thoughts and actions are healed and the person can make a new start.

Oil is also seen as a sign of Jesus as 'King' and of his power and ability to rule over the world. In the past, important people such as kings and queens were anointed with oil when they were crowned. Oil is still used in some coronation ceremonies today.

Some Christians' thoughts today

'To me the cross is the most important symbol. It points the way to heaven and reminds me there is life after death.'

'When I take the bread and wine it reminds me of the sacrifice Jesus made.'

'Fifteen years ago I was very ill and given only six months to live. I was anointed with oil during a healing service. I see oil as a symbol of God's love and his power and ability to help and heal us.'

The symbol of the fish

The symbol of the fish is one of the oldest Christian symbols. In the early Church, when it was dangerous to be a Christian, followers would draw a fish in the sand outside a house where a meeting was to take place. The last person to enter would rub it out with their feet.

The fish symbol can be seen on the graves in the Catacombs in Rome, where Christians used to meet in secret. Today, some people wear a fish badge or have a sticker on their car to show that they are Christians.

The symbol of the fish reminds Christians that Jesus told his disciples to be 'fishers of men', and that he fed 5000 people with five loaves and two small fish.

How Christians use symbols

In this section you will:

- find out more about Christian symbols
- look at how Christians use symbols to express their beliefs and ideas
- read about the symbols used by the Salvation Army.

Some **Christian denominations** use very few symbols in worship because they believe that symbols stop people from thinking about God. Others think that symbols help people to concentrate on God. What Christians believe about the use of symbols affects the shape of church buildings and the objects inside.

Some churches have been built in the shape of a **cross**. Others are very plain, ordinary buildings. In some churches, **incense** is burnt and the rising smoke symbolizes the prayers going up to God.

Flowers in church are symbols of love and devotion from the people who put them there. Lighted candles symbolize goodness, knowledge and truth.

Christians use symbolic language, metaphors and imagery, to describe Jesus or God. They do this because it is very difficult for them to say exactly what God or Jesus is like. For example, some call Jesus the 'Light of the World' because they believe he showed people the way out of darkness and evil and into a new life.

Actions during worship can be symbolic. Some Christians bend their right knee or bow when they pass in front of the altar and as they enter and leave the church. This is called **genuflection** and it symbolizes respect for God. There is symbolic meaning in how Christians choose to pray. Kneeling down and bowing their heads shows **humility**, which means they know that God is much greater and more important than they are. Standing up to pray shows respect. Sometimes, Christians lie flat on the floor to pray with their arms outstretched (prostrate). This shows that they are prepared to do whatever God asks of them.

During some services, as a sign of peace, Christians give each other a hug or shake hands. Sometimes the **priest** places their hands on a persons' head or body as a symbol of God's blessing and healing. Christians call this 'laying on of hands'.

You can often tell what job a person does in the church by what they wear. The priest often wears a white 'dog collar'. This collar resembles the neck halter worn by slaves. It symbolizes that priests are not their own masters but do God's work.

Some Churches, such as the Greek Orthodox Church, burn incense during their services

Members of the Salvation Army

The colours are linked to festivals, which are based on events in Jesus' life.

Colour is also linked to certain services and ceremonies. White is a symbol of purity and people who are being baptized or confirmed usually wear something white. A Christian bride often wears white at her wedding. When people go to funerals they often wear black or dark colours to symbolize sadness and grief.

Monks and nuns also wear special clothes, which shows they have given their lives to God and His work. Christians who belong to the **Salvation Army** wear smart uniforms. This symbolizes their belief that as Christians they should live an ordered and disciplined life as a soldier does.

In some Churches, the colour of the **vestments**, special clothes worn by priests during services, and the cloths which cover the altar, change with the Church calendar.

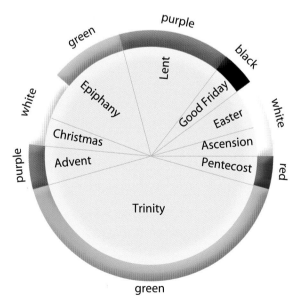

The Christian Church has different seasons, represented by various colours

The Salvation Army

William Booth founded the Salvation Army in the East End of London in 1878 CE.

The Salvation Army crest is full of symbolism, and so is their motto: 'Blood and Fire'. The 'Blood' refers to the death and sacrifice of Jesus, and the 'Fire' refers to how the **Holy Spirit** came to Jesus' disciples ('tongues of fire').

The crest shows a cross with an 'S' wrapped around it to represent **salvation**. The two crossed swords represent the battle against **sin**. The rays symbolize the power of the Holy Spirit, and the crown symbolizes the glory of being rewarded by God for following His ways.

Worship

In this section you will:
- learn about Christian worship
- find out why Christians worship God
- study the main features of a Christian church
- read about the Roman Catholic practice of confession.

Taking part in worship is very important to **Christians** for the following reasons:

- to show their love for God
- to thank or to praise God
- to show that they want to live and behave as God wants them to
- to ask God for help and guidance in their daily lives
- to ask God for forgiveness
- to strengthen their faith and become closer to God.

Where do Christians worship?

Christians can worship God anywhere, on their own or with other people. They can go to a building, a place of worship. The building may be a **church** but it may also be a hall, a private home, a chapel, a citadel, a minster or a cathedral. Christians can worship on any day of the week, but the special day for worship is a Sunday. This is chosen because Sunday is their **holy** day. Christians believe that Jesus rose from the dead on a Sunday.

The majority of Christians worship in a church. There are thousands of churches all over the world. In Christianity, the word 'church' has two meanings. 'Church' with a capital 'C' means the different **denominations** of the Christian community. The word 'church' with a small 'c' means the building in which many Christians worship.

Christians treat their place of worship and all the objects inside it with great respect. They believe churches are sacred (holy) places.

What do churches look like?

Many churches were built in the shape of a **cross**. They were built facing east in the direction of the rising sun. The rising sun

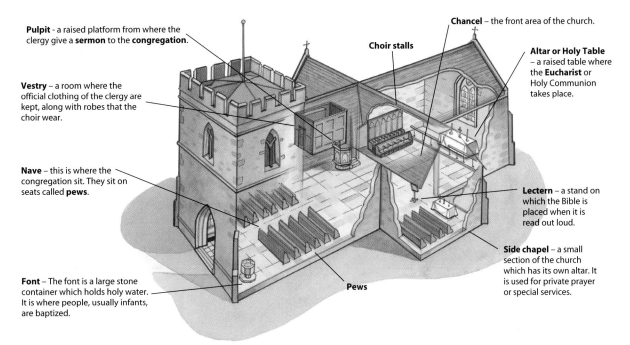

Pulpit - a raised platform from where the clergy give a **sermon** to the **congregation**.

Chancel – the front area of the church.

Choir stalls

Altar or Holy Table – a raised table where the **Eucharist** or Holy Communion takes place.

Vestry – a room where the official clothing of the clergy are kept, along with robes that the choir wear.

Nave – this is where the congregation sit. They sit on seats called **pews**.

Lectern – a stand on which the Bible is placed when it is read out loud.

Side chapel – a small section of the church which has its own altar. It is used for private prayer or special services.

Font – The font is a large stone container which holds holy water. It is where people, usually infants, are baptized.

Pews

The main features of an Anglican Church

symbolizes light and life at the start of a new day. East is also the direction of Jerusalem, where Christians believe that Jesus died and rose from the dead. Modern-day churches have been built in many different shapes and sizes and sometimes other buildings have been made into churches.

Modern churches often have the altar in the middle of the church. This symbolizes that the **priest** and ordinary people who go to church (the **laity**) are all involved in the worship. Most Anglican and Roman Catholic churches are very similar in design.

Confession

Roman Catholics follow the practice of **confession**. This means that they confess, or tell, their sins to the priest. They do this is in a confessional. Two small cubicles are linked by a grille, so the priests can hear, but not see, the person on the other side. After confession, the priest tells them to say special prayers to show they are sorry.

The tabernacle

On or near the altar in Roman Catholic churches, you will see the tabernacle. This is a small cupboard shaped like a tent. Inside are kept the bread or wafers which have been **consecrated** (made holy) ready for the **Eucharist**. A light is always burning in front of the tabernacle to symbolize that God is always there.

There are 14 pictures in the walls, which tell the story of Jesus' crucifixion. These are called the Stations of the Cross.

Ways of worshipping

In this section you will:

- learn about how Christians worship God
- find out about the different ways Christians worship and look at some of the things they use to help them worship
- read about what happens during the Eucharist service.

How do Christians worship?

Some **Christians** prefer a formal, set service. The worship follows a set pattern of rituals or actions called a **liturgy**. This kind of worship is colourful and dramatic and full of symbols, such as carrying the **cross** at the start of the service. People taking part in the worship make symbolic actions such as kneeling to pray. Most Churches have all this written down in a book which worshippers follow during the service.

Other Christians choose to worship in a much less formal way. Worship does not follow a set pattern and the emphasis is on the Bible and on the words spoken by the **clergy** or leaders of the worship. Hymns, prayers, Bible readings and **sermons**, which are talks given by the clergy, are all important aspects of worship.

Many Christians believe that their everyday lives should be an act of worship. This means remembering and being thankful to God in all that they do and doing their very best.

The Eucharist or Holy Communion

The most important set service for Christians is the **Eucharist** or Holy Communion. During this service Christians remember the final meal that Jesus had with his **disciples**, known as the **Last Supper**. They share in a symbolic meal of bread and wine. The bread is a symbol of Jesus' body and the wine a symbol of his blood. Different **denominations** call this service by different names and celebrate it in different ways.

The Eucharist is a very special service called a **sacrament**. Christians believe that they receive special blessings from God during a sacrament. There are seven sacraments: **baptism**, the Eucharist, **confirmation**, **marriage**, **confession**, **ordination** (when a person becomes a priest) and **Anointing of the sick**. Sacraments are especially important to Roman Catholics.

Aids to worship

Different Christian denominations use different things to help them worship. Look at the list below to find out about some of the things they might use.

Actions
Worshippers carry out actions which show their beliefs and feelings. They may clap, dance, sway or kneel. They may also shake hands or give each other a hug as a sign of God's peace.

The Bible
Passages are read from the Bible during most services.

Bread and wine

Christians share bread and wine during some services. Jesus asked the disciples to do this in memory of him. The bread symbolizes his body and the wine symbolizes his blood.

Candles

Christians believe that candles show the goodness and love of God shining in a dark and sinful world.

Cross

The **cross** is the main symbol of Christianity. It helps worshippers to remember that Jesus rose from the dead.

Crucifix

A **crucifix** is a cross with an image of Jesus on it. It helps to remind Christians of the suffering and sacrifice of Jesus.

Icons

An icon is a holy picture of Jesus, his mother the **Virgin Mary**, or another Christian **saint**. Some Christians believe that Jesus and the saints are with God and can speak to God on their behalf. Icons are mainly used by Orthodox Christians and are believed to be very holy. They are carried in procession at festivals.

Incense

Incense is a gum or spice. When it is burnt, it gives off sweet-smelling smoke. The incense container or censer is swung from a chain during worship. As the smoke rises Christians believe their prayers also rise up to God.

Music

Music is an important part of worship and a range of instruments are played. Music often accompanies hymns, **psalms** and other prayers and religious songs.

Rosary

A rosary is a string of beads with a crucifix on the end. They are mainly used by Roman Catholics who pass the beads between their finger and thumb as they pray.

Service book

A service book sets out the order of service. It tells the worshipper what to do and say.

Silence

Silence helps the worshippers to focus and concentrate on God.

Singing

Worshippers express their feelings and beliefs by singing.

Statues

These are usually of the saints, such as the Virgin Mary. Worshippers pray and light candles in front of the statues. They believe that the saints are already with God and can speak for them.

The Eucharist service

The Eucharist, or Holy Communion, is the most holy of all Christian services. It reminds people of the Last Supper which Jesus shared with his disciples, when he asked them to eat bread and drink wine together in memory of him. Jesus said that the bread represents his body and that the wine represents his blood.

During the service, worshippers sing hymns and say special prayers. They ask for forgiveness for all the things they have done wrong. Passages are read from the Bible, and the **priest** gives a talk, called a sermon. Bread (or small wafers) and wine is blessed, and each worshipper is given a piece of bread and a sip of wine. In some Churches, the bread is dipped in the wine before it is given to the worshippers. At the end of the service, the priest will give a blessing and, in some Churches, the worshippers are told, 'Go in peace to love and serve the Lord.'

Prayer

In this section you will:

- learn about Christian prayer
- find out why Christians pray and look at different kinds of prayer
- read about and reflect upon the prayer Jesus taught his **disciples**, now called the Lord's Prayer.

When **Christians** pray they talk to God. To them, **prayer** is a way of talking and listening to God. Prayer is very important to Christians. Many Christians think about Jesus or God as their best friend and have a personal relationship by talking to God through prayer.

How and why do Christians pray?

Christians pray in many different ways. They can pray on their own or in a group. They may say prayers 'inside their head' or they may say them out loud. They may say prayers which are written down as part of a service, or they may make them up. Christians may stand up to pray, or they may kneel down or just sit. They may close their eyes and put their hands together or they may not.

Christians believe in the 'power of prayer'. They believe that prayer can change things and that when they pray it brings them closer to God.

Christians are taught to love and pray for their enemies (Matthew 5: 44)

'One of the reasons I pray is:

… to say sorry for the things I have done wrong and ask God to forgive me

… to tell God He is important to me

… because I want God to know that I love Him

… to try to be a better person

… to ask God to help me and other people who need help

… because Jesus told us to

… to say thank you to God for all the good things in my life

… to find out what God wants me to do.'

What kind of prayers do Christians use?

There are five main forms of prayer that Christians use.

1 *Adoration* – this is when Christians pray about God's greatness and power and remember how special and important God is.

2 *Confession* – this is when Christians say they are sorry for all the things they have done wrong and ask God to forgive them.

3 *Intercession* – this is when Christians pray for other people and ask God to help or guide them.

4 *Petition* – this is when Christians ask for God's help and guidance for themselves.

5 *Thanksgiving* – this is when Christians say thank you for all that God has given them and done for them.

Meditation is another kind of prayer. When someone is meditating they are very still and quiet. They try hard not to think about anything except God.

The Lord's Prayer is one of the best-known Christian prayers. Christians believe that Jesus taught his disciples this prayer. We can read it in the Matthew 6: 9–13. It is used during most acts of Christian worship.

The Lords' Prayer

In Matthew's **Gospel** in the **New Testament**, it tells how Jesus taught his disciples to pray quietly and privately. He taught them a special prayer, which is now called the Lord's Prayer. It is used in Christian Churches everywhere.

'Our Father in Heaven
Hallowed be your name
Your kingdom come
Your will be done,
On earth as it is in heaven
Give us this day our daily bread.
Forgive us our sins
As we forgive those who sin against us.
Lead us not into temptation
but deliver us from evil.
For the kingdom, the power and the glory are yours
Now and for ever. Amen'

Festivals

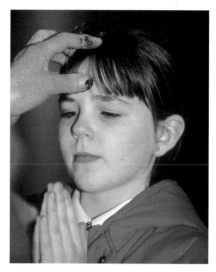

A cross of ash is made on a young worshipper's forehead

Birthdays and anniversaries are festivals. They are days when celebrations take place. These are called **secular** or non-religious festivals. Religious festivals remember an important religious event in the past. The main **Christian** festivals are based on the life of Jesus. These festivals happen every year. Some festivals last for a day, others for longer. Some Christian **denominations** think that certain festivals are more important than others. All Christians celebrate the festivals of Christmas and Easter.

The date of Christian festivals can change from year to year. This is because festivals depend on the date of **Easter Day**, which is the Sunday after the full moon at the end of March. Only two festivals are on the same day each year, Christmas and Epiphany.

Epiphany – 6 January

At Epiphany, Christians remember when the Wise Men or Magi from the East came to visit the baby Jesus. Epiphany is the last day of the Christmas festival and the day when most people take down their Christmas decorations.

Ash Wednesday – February/March

Ash Wednesday is a day when Christians show that they are sorry for all the things they have done wrong. Many go to church and the **priest** will smear a **cross** of ash on their forehead. Ash Wednesday marks the beginning of Lent, when Christians remember the time that Jesus spent in the wilderness.

Easter – March/April

Easter is the most important festival in the Christian **Church**. The festival begins on **Good Friday**, when Christians remember that Jesus died on the cross. It ends on Easter Sunday when they celebrate their belief that Jesus rose from the dead.

Trinity Sunday – May/June

This is when Christians celebrate their belief that God has made himself known to the world in three ways: God the Father, God the Son and God the Holy Spirit.

Christmas – 25 December

Christmas is when Christians celebrate the birth of Jesus, but no one really knows when he was born. The celebration of Christmas lasts for twelve days and ends with Epiphany.

'… He was taken up to Heaven as they watched Him…' (Acts 1: 9)

Ascension Day – May/June

Ascension Day is when Christians celebrate their belief that 40 days after he rose from the dead (the **resurrection**), Jesus went back up to Heaven to be with God.

Pentecost – May/June

Pentecost is when Christians celebrate the start of the Christian Church. The **New Testament** tells us that there was a sound 'like a strong wind blowing' and 'tongues of fire which spread out … They were all filled with the **Holy Spirit**'. (Acts 2: 2–4) The **disciples** went out and began spreading the 'good news' about Jesus. In this country, Pentecost is also called Whitsun, or 'White Sunday'. This is because it used to be a popular day for **baptisms** and many people wore white as a sign of purity.

Key Christian festivals

- *Epiphany.* This remembers the visit of the wise men to the baby Jesus.

- *Ash Wednesday.* This is when Christians say they are sorry for things they have done wrong.

- *Easter.* This celebrates Jesus rising from the dead.

- *Ascension Day.* This remembers when Jesus went back to heaven to be with God.

- *Pentecost.* This remembers the gift of the Holy Spirit given to Jesus' disciples.

- *Trinity.* This celebrates that God is one God but three persons: the Father, the Son and the Holy Spirit.

- *Christmas.* This celebrates Jesus' birth.

Christmas and Easter

In this section you will:
- learn about what Christmas and Easter mean to Christians
- find out how they prepare for and celebrate Christmas
- read about St Nicholas, a popular Christian saint in many countries.

Easter and Christmas are the two most important festivals in Christianity.

Christmas celebrates the birth of Jesus, when God came to live on earth as a human being.

Easter is the greatest of all **Christian** festivals. It remembers Jesus' death and celebrates the Christian belief that Jesus rose from the dead.

Christians believe that Jesus' life and death was for a reason. They believe that before Jesus came, human beings had forgotten about God and lived selfish lives, doing many wrong things and not thinking of others. Christians say that Jesus changed things and made it possible for humans to know God better. He taught them about God and the way God wanted them to live. Christians believe that His death made up for all the wrong things they had done in the past and brought them closer to God.

Christians call the day Jesus died **Good Friday** because they believe something very good happened as a result of his death.

The **resurrection**, when Jesus rose from the dead, has several meanings for Christians. They believe it proves that Jesus was the Son of God, that he is 'alive' today and that it is proof that there is life after death. They also see it as a sign of God's **forgiveness**.

Jesus is sometimes called the **Redeemer** or the **Saviour**. Christians say He is the Redeemer because He 'brought people back' to God. They say He is the Saviour because He saved people from sin and death by dying on the cross and rising from the dead.

How do Christians celebrate Christmas?

The four weeks before Christmas are called **Advent**. The word 'advent' means 'coming'. Advent is the time when Christians get ready for Christmas. They think about Jesus coming into the world as a baby and about what this means. Christians believe that Jesus was the **Messiah**, a saviour sent by God to bring goodness and peace to the world.

Counting the weeks until Christmas

The church is decorated for Christmas

During Advent, Christians read parts of the **Old Testament** of the Bible which talk about what the Messiah will be like. They also think about the future because Jesus promised that he would come again and judge who will or will not go to Heaven to be with God. Christians call this the **Second Coming**.

Carols are sung during the Christmas celebrations. A carol is a song celebrating the birth of Jesus. Some Christians light Advent candles or open Advent calendars to count the days to Christmas. Houses and many churches are decorated with Christmas trees and lights. Christmas is sometimes called a festival of light because it celebrates the birth of Jesus who Christians call 'the light of the world'. Christians also believe that Jesus was God's gift to the world and this is where the idea of giving presents comes from.

Most Christians try to go to church at Christmas. One of the most popular services is **Midnight Mass** which starts at about 11.30pm. They sing carols and take part in the **Eucharist**.

What do Christians say about Christmas?

'… Many people have forgotten the real meaning of Christmas… it's not about tinsel, selection boxes and presents… it's about Jesus!'

'… I especially try to follow Jesus' example at Christmas… I think about people who are not as lucky as I am and try to help them.'

'… At Christmas I say thank you to God for Jesus.'

St Nicholas

St Nicholas is a popular Christian **saint**. In Britain, nearly 500 churches are dedicated to him. In Advent, on 6 December, Christians remember St Nicholas. Santa Claus and Father Christmas are based on St Nicholas, who is remembered for being kind and generous, and for taking care of people less fortunate than himself.

There is a story about St Nicholas and why children hang up stockings at Christmas. There was once a poor man whose daughters could not marry because he had no money to give them. One night, without telling anyone, St Nicholas dropped bags of gold down the chimney of their cottage. The gold fell into their stockings which were hanging up to dry by the fireplace. This is why children today hang up their stockings at Christmas, hoping that they will be filled with good things.

Easter

In this section you will:
- find out how Christians prepare for and celebrate Easter
- be able to think about giving something up for a good reason
- read about street carnivals, called Mardi Gras, which take place before Lent.

A Palm Sunday procession

How do Christians celebrate Easter?

The time before Easter, is called Lent. Lent starts on Ash Wednesday and lasts for 40 days ending on **Easter Sunday**. **Christians** believe that Jesus spent 40 days and nights in the desert being tempted by the Devil before he started his ministry. Lent is a time for Christians to think about their own lives and is a serious time for the Christian **Church**.

The day before the start of Lent is Shrove Tuesday which is often called 'Pancake Day'. Long ago, Christians followed a very strict plain diet during Lent and so the day before it started, they used up all the rich food they had left. This included eggs, milk and flour which were made into pancakes. Today, many Christians give up something they like eating, such as chocolate, during Lent.

The last week of Lent is known as **Holy Week**. This is when Christians remember the last seven days of Jesus' life. It starts on **Palm Sunday** and includes **Maundy Thursday**, **Good Friday** and **Holy Saturday**.

On Palm Sunday Christians remember the time when Jesus rode into Jerusalem on a donkey. The crowd gave him a great welcome. They waved palm leaves in the air and laid them on the ground for the donkey to walk on. Many Churches give out palm crosses on Palm Sunday. Some Christians take part in processions, where they walk behind a donkey waving palm branches or crosses and singing hymns.

Maundy Thursday is when Christians remember the **Last Supper** which Jesus had with his disciples before his arrest in the garden of Gethsemane. In some Christian communities the **priest** will wash the feet of the worshippers. This is

Russian Orthodox Christians kiss the coffin of Christ on Good Friday

because at the Last Supper Jesus washed the feet of his disciples to show that everyone is equal in God's eyes.

Good Friday is the saddest day in the Christian year, when Christians remember that Jesus was crucified. Churches are stripped of all their decorations and everything is very dull and dark. Many Christians go to church between the hours of 12.00pm and 3.00pm which is the time when Jesus is believed to have hung on the cross. Some churches also take part in processions and carry a big **cross**, or hold a sort of funeral service for Jesus.

Holy Saturday is the last day of Lent. The church is cleaned and decorated with beautiful flowers. At night Christians go to church to take part in the Easter Vigil. The word 'vigil' means 'to keep watch'. The service starts in darkness except for some candles so that the Bible can be read. The worshippers then light their own candles from a special candle called the **paschal candle** and the church is filled with light. The paschal candle represents Jesus as the light of the world.

Easter Day is a joyful day when Christians celebrate the **resurrection**, their belief that Jesus rose from the dead. Christians make a special effort to go to church on Easter Sunday and to take part in the **Eucharist**. For some Christians, the celebrations begin at dawn with a bonfire. They also hard boil eggs and paint them. The eggs are symbols of new life and chocolate Easter eggs come from this idea.

What do Christians say about Easter?

'… On Good Friday I mourn Jesus. I feel his pain and suffering. On Easter Sunday I feel happy. I know that Jesus is alive…'

'… Easter reminds me that there is life after death. I think about people I have known who have died… and I feel happy to think that I will see them again one day.'

Mardi Gras

In some Roman Catholic communities, there is a big celebration in the week before Lent. Street carnivals, called Mardi Gras, which is French for 'Fat Tuesday', are held in places such as Cologne in Germany, Nice in France and Rio de Janeiro in Brazil. There are wonderful parades, with colourful floats and costumes, and parties and dancing in the streets.

The word 'carnival' comes from an old Italian word, *carnelevare*, which means the removal of meat. Mardi Gras is the last chance for some Christians to eat meat. They will not have any more meat until the end of Lent, which is six weeks away.

Pilgrimage 1

A **pilgrim** is someone who goes on a religious journey called a **pilgrimage**. Pilgrims visit places which are thought to be **holy** or sacred. This may be where a miracle is believed to have happened, or where an important religious leader or teacher was born or is buried.

Christians do not have to go on a pilgrimage. It is their free choice.

People go on pilgrimages for different reasons:

● to show they are Christians

● to become closer to God

● to say thank you for something good that has happened

● to make up for something they have done wrong – Christians call this **penance**

● to ask for help or healing

● to find out what it is like.

Pilgrimages can also be 'inner journeys', when Christians think about their real self and what God wants of them.

To find out more about themselves and God, some Christians go on a retreat. This is a special kind of pilgrimage. Most retreats take place in Christian surroundings such as monasteries, but they can take place anywhere that is quiet and peaceful.

Where do Christians go on pilgrimages?

There are many Christian holy places all over the world. Most of them are 'official' places of pilgrimage. This means that the leaders of the Christian **Church** believe that something special happened there.

The Holy Land

The tomb of Christ in the Church of the Holy Sepulchre, Jerusalem, is an important pilgrimage site for Christians

Many Christian choose to make a pilgrimage to Israel, which is where Jesus lived. They visit places such as Bethlehem, where Jesus was born, and Nazareth where he grew up. They also visit the area around the Sea of Galilee where Jesus performed miracles and taught people about God, and Jerusalem where he was crucified and rose from the dead.

Rome

Many Christians make a pilgrimage to Rome in Italy. Rome was the centre of the early Church and many Christians, including Peter and Paul, died for their faith in Rome. Pilgrims can visit the Catacombs, which are underground burial tombs. This is where the early Christians used to meet and worship in secret. Pilgrims can also visit several famous buildings, such as the Vatican, where the **Pope** lives. The Pope is the leader of the Roman Catholic Church. St Peter's Basilica is also in Rome. It is a beautiful church built on the site where Peter was buried. There is a **shrine** inside dedicated to him.

Millions of pilgrims visit Lourdes every year to pray and receive healing

Lourdes

In 1858, a fourteen-year-old French girl called Bernadette Soubirous said she saw Jesus' mother, the **Virgin Mary**, at Lourdes in France. It is claimed that the Virgin Mary asked for a chapel to be built. She also told Bernadette to dig in the mud and a spring of water bubbled up. Many people claim to have been healed from all kinds of illnesses and disabilities after bathing in the spring water. Millions of Christians visit Lourdes every year to pray and be healed.

Egeria's pilgrimage

Hundreds of Christians from Europe went on pilgrimages to the Holy Land, which is modern-day Israel, in 385–1099 CE. Some of these pilgrims wrote about their experiences, and eighteen of these accounts have survived.

One is by a woman called Egeria, who went on pilgrimage to the Holy Land in the fourth century CE. She kept a journal about her travels, which tells us a great deal about how the early Christian church was organized and what Jerusalem looked like in those days. She wrote down lots of information about the places she visited, and described in detail what she saw and felt.

Egeria's journal shows that she loved God very much. It tells us that she stopped at different places on her pilgrimage to read Bible passages about each place, and to give thanks.

Pilgrimage 2

In this section you will:
- look at some places of Christian pilgrimage
- learn about the Taizé community in France.

Fatima

Fatima is in Portugal. Many Roman Catholic **Christians** make a **pilgrimage** to Fatima because they believe that in 1917 three children saw the **Virgin Mary** there. The children were Lucia de Jesus, aged ten, and her cousins Francisco and Jacinta Marto, aged nine and seven. They described the vision as a 'Lady more brilliant than the sun'. The 'Lady' told Lucia three secrets, called the Secrets of Fatima.

The first secret was a vision of hell, believed to be the two World Wars. The second secret was a vision of peace. The third secret has not been fully revealed. The Roman Catholic **Church** says it is about suffering and people dying for their faith.

Pilgrims who go to Fatima sometimes crawl on their knees to the **shrine** to show that they are sorry for all their **sins**. Pilgrims buy large candles and light them to remind them of someone who needs God's help. These candles are then thrown into a big furnace and a prayer is said.

Walsingham

Christians from different **denominations** go on pilgrimages to Walsingham in England because a lady called Richeldis de Faverches is believed to have seen a vision of the Virgin Mary there in 1061. Jesus' mother showed Richeldis what Jesus' home in Nazareth looked like and Richeldis built a replica of the house she saw in her vision. When pilgrims visit the **Holy** House, they think about when Jesus was a boy, living as part of an ordinary family although he was the Son of God.

Medjugorje

Medjugorje in Bosnia is a modern, 'unofficial' pilgrimage site. Pilgrims have been going to Medjugorje since 1981 when six young people in the village claimed to have seen the Virgin Mary there. Since that time they claim to have seen her more than 300 times. They say that her purpose is to guide people back to God.

Many retreats are held in Christian settings such as a monastery or abbey

Iona

Iona is a small island off the west coast of Scotland. It is a place of pilgrimage and retreat. St Columba, who was an Irish prince and also a Christian, went to live on Iona in 563 CE when he was forced to leave Ireland. Today, Iona is an **ecumenical** Christian community. This means that Christians of all denominations live and worship there together as a symbol of Christian unity. The community has 240 members from all kinds of backgrounds. They don't have to stay on Iona all the time but they must follow the rules of Iona wherever they are. They must:

● take part in regular worship and pray for half an hour each morning

● be prepared to share what they have with others

● account for the way they spend their time and their money

● meet with other community members (three times a year on the mainland and for a week in the summer on Iona)

● work for justice and peace.

Ordinary Christians can spend time on Iona. They can go to work there for a time or go as pilgrims on retreat. The community runs a youth organization, and young people can go there during their holidays. Most people return home feeling rested and closer to God.

Taizé

Taizé is a Christian community in eastern France which was set up in 1940 by a monk called Brother Roger. He wanted to bring together Christians from all denominations so that they could learn to gain a better understanding about each other's beliefs.

Today, Taizé is a place of pilgrimage for hundreds of thousands of people, especially young adults. Not all the visitors are Christian, but everyone is welcome if they want to work for peace and understanding amongst all peoples. Many visitors stay for a week and live as part of the community. They can choose from several ways to spend the week, including being silent.

Prayer and music play an important part in daily life of the Taizé community and prayers usually start and end the day for everyone. Many churches use Taizé songs in their worship.

Baptism

In this section you will:

● learn about the different stages and ceremonies in a Christian's life

● find out why baptism is important to Christians and what happens during an infant baptism

● read and think about when Jesus was baptized in the River Jordan.

Believers' baptisms are happy and joyous occasions

Christians believe that God gives them life when they are born and that they go back to God when they die. Many see life as a **pilgrimage**, a journey 'from the cradle to the grave'. **Rites of passage** are special ceremonies which mark important events along the way. They are called rites of passage because the ceremonies have rituals (or rites).

The four main Christian rites of passage are **baptism**, **confirmation**, **marriage** and death. Many Christians, who believe that they receive special blessings from God during these ceremonies, also call baptism, confirmation and marriage **sacraments**.

Baptism

The first rite of passage is baptism. Christians believe that this is an important ceremony when people of all ages become members of the Christian **Church**. Jesus was baptized in the river Jordan by His cousin, John the Baptist,

before he started his ministry. Jesus told his **disciples** to baptize others (Matthew 28: 19), and so Christians believe that they are doing as he asked when they are baptized. Baptism marks the beginning of a persons' life as a Christian.

What happens during baptism?

Baptism takes place in a church. It may be part of an ordinary service or a private ceremony. Some Churches baptize babies. This is called infant baptism, or christening. The word christening comes from the idea that, during the service, the baby is given their 'Christian' name as part of Christ's family. Babies often wear white clothes as a symbol of purity and goodness.

At a baby's baptism, the parents and godparents gather around the font and make promises. The parents name the child and the vicar or **priest** makes the sign of the **cross** on the baby's forehead.

Holy Water, from the font, is poured over the baby's head three times. This represents the **Trinity**, or three aspects of God: Father, Son and **Holy Spirit**.

Water is a very important symbol in baptism. Water poured over the baby's head is a symbol of washing away **sins** which happened before the baby was born. Christians call this original sin. This comes from the idea that the first human beings disobeyed God and their sins have been passed on to every human being since that time. In Roman Catholic baptisms the baby has holy oil smeared on its chest and head. This is called anointing with oil. In the Orthodox Church babies (and adults) are totally immersed in water three times to symbolize the belief in the Trinity, the death of past sins and new life in Jesus.

At the end of the ceremony some Churches give the parents a lighted candle. This shows that the baby is now part of the Christian family and belongs to Jesus.

Believer's baptism

Some **denominations**, such as the Baptist and Pentecostal Churches, do not baptize babies. Babies are welcomed into the church with a special service of dedication, but people are only baptized when they decide for themselves as an adult. This is called a **believer's baptism**. During the service, people being baptized make public promises (vows) and commit themselves to being Christians. They are then immersed in water, a symbol of washing away sin and the start of a new life.

Believer's baptisms usually take place in a church, which has a **baptistry**. This is a small pool just big enough for a person to be lowered under the water. Baptisms can also take place in the sea or in a river or even in a swimming pool. Many Christians want to be baptized in the River Jordan in Israel, which is where Jesus was baptized.

The baptism of Jesus

In the **Gospels** in the **New Testament**, we read about what happened when Jesus was baptized by his cousin, who was known as John the Baptist. John had been telling people that they must change their ways and start a new life, living as God wanted them to. He baptized people in the River Jordan to symbolize the washing away of sin, and he told them about Jesus: 'I baptized you with water, but he will baptize you with the Holy Spirit'.

One day, Jesus came to John and asked to be baptized. At first, John said that he could not do it, because Jesus was much more important than him, but Jesus persuaded him that it was what God wanted. John told the people, 'Behold the lamb of God who comes to take away the sins of the world.'

The Gospels say that when Jesus came out of the river, a dove came down and rested on him, and a voice from heaven said, 'This is my beloved Son, in whom I am well pleased.'

Confirmation

In this section you will:

● learn about a Christian **rite of passage** called confirmation

● find out why confirmation is important to Christians and what happens during a confirmation service

● learn about differences in confirmation practices in different Churches.

Confirmation is when **Christians** become full adult members of the **Church**. When they were baptized as a baby, other people made promises for them. When they are confirmed they make their own promises. Many people believe that confirmation brings them closer to God and that they get strength and guidance from the **Holy Spirit**. In some Churches being confirmed means that you accept the bread and wine in the **Eucharist** service.

When are people confirmed?

There is no set age for confirmation. Roman Catholics are usually confirmed and take their first communion at about eight years old. In the Church of England many people are confirmed as teenagers.

Young Roman Catholics taking their first Holy Communion

The laying on of hands during confirmation is a symbol of blessing

People preparing for confirmation usually attend classes run by their local church. This helps them to understand what is expected of them as Christians.

Confirmation services are usually performed by a bishop. The person being confirmed must answer questions such as, 'Do you believe and trust in God?' The bishop lays his hands on each person's head and prays that the Holy Spirit will guide them and make them strong in their faith. In some Churches, the bishop will put oil on the person's forehead to symbolize the gifts and blessings that the Holy Spirit will bring.

In Orthodox Churches there is no separate service of confirmation. A service called chrismation follows straight after the **baptism** service and oil is smeared on the baby's eyes, lips, nostrils, mouth and forehead as well as the chest, hands and feet. This is a symbol that being a Christian involves the whole person.

Churches that carry out **believer's baptisms** do not have confirmation services. The baptism itself is like a confirmation because people are making their own promises, having decided to be full members of the Christian Church.

What do Christians say about confirmation?

'I decided to get confirmed when I was thirteen. It was the first really big decision that I had made about my life… I wanted God to know that I was choosing to be a Christian and not just following the tradition of my parents.'

'I enjoyed going to church but I always felt that something was missing because I could never take bread and wine during the Eucharist. After I got confirmed, I really felt part of the community.'

Confirmation

The word 'confirm' means to verify or to make stronger. The Christian rite of passage called confirmation means that Christians can make their faith stronger by confirming promises made for them when they were babies.

Roman Catholics believe that when children are about eight years old, they are able to make and keep promises for themselves. They go to special classes to be taught by the **priest** about what being a Roman Catholic means and about the responsibilities they have once they take their first communion (Eucharist).

In the Anglican Church, confirmation usually takes place later, during the teenage years, but the young people also attend preparation classes led by the priest. There is no age limit to becoming a Christian. People can be baptized and confirmed at any age.

Marriage and funerals

In this section you will:
- learn why marriage is important to Christians
- find out what happens during a Christian marriage ceremony and funeral ceremony
- read about 'last rites' for Roman Catholics.

Marriage

Christians say that **marriage** is a gift or a blessing from God. They believe that God brings two people together to support each other through life. Christians see marriage as the right relationship for having sexual intercourse and children.

Before they get married, many couples attend marriage courses run by their **church**. This helps them to understand the Christian teaching on marriage and the importance of the marriage vows.

What happens during a Christian marriage ceremony?

All marriage ceremonies have some features in common.

- The ceremony usually begins with a hymn.
- The purpose of Christian marriage is explained and the guests are asked if there is any reason why the marriage cannot take place.
- Once the **priest** or vicar is sure that there are no objections, the couple make vows (promises) to each other and exchange rings. Christians believe that they are making these vows before God.
- The priest tells everyone the couple are now 'husband and wife' and prayers are said for them.
- Last of all, the bride and groom sign the marriage register to record that the marriage is legal.

Wedding rings are usually complete circles with no beginning or end. They symbolize that marriage vows cannot be broken.

In Orthodox Churches, when couples have made their vows and exchanged rings, crowns or garlands of flowers are placed on their heads as symbols that the couple has been blessed by God. They also drink wine from the same cup to show they are starting a new life together. Finally, the priest leads the couple in a circle around the church to symbolize that the marriage will have no end.

The bride and groom kneel while the priest blesses them

Death

What happens during a Christian funeral?

Christians believe in life after death. This idea is called **eternal life**.

Christians believe that when someone dies they pass from this life to the next and go to be with God where they will live forever. Their belief that Jesus died and rose from the dead and went back to God, brings comfort to them. They believe that one day, when they die, they will meet Jesus and be with their loved ones in Heaven.

Funeral services take place in a church or a **crematorium** chapel. Most people wear dark clothes as a symbol of sadness and grief. The service usually has hymns, prayers, readings and a **sermon** or talk about death and the **resurrection** and the life of the person who has died. After the service, the body is cremated or buried in a consecrated (blessed) graveyard. This final part of the service is called the committal.

Last rites

Many churches have special services or rituals which can take place before a person dies. These are called the 'last rites'.

When someone who is a Roman Catholic is dying, they may ask a priest to give them the last rites. The priest will hear their last confession and (representing God) will forgive them all their sins so that they may die in peace. He will anoint (smear) their eyes, ears, nostrils, mouth and hands with holy oil, and give them the last communion (**Eucharist**) of bread and wine. This is usually a small wafer dipped in wine, which symbolizes food for the journey from death to everlasting life.

One way Christians remember their loved ones who have died is by dedicating a headstone to them

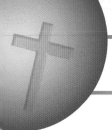

Creation

In this section you will:
- look at Christian beliefs about creation
- learn how Christians believe the universe began
- read about Charles Darwin.

What do Christians believe about creation?

Christians believe that God created the world and all that is in it. They say the wonders of the world, the beauty of nature and the solar system did not happen by chance. The creation story in the book of Genesis explains what many Christians think happened when the world began.

On the second day God made the sky. He used the sky to divide the water that covered the Earth into two halves.

On the third day God made land beneath the water. He called the land 'earth' and the water the 'sea'. God also made plants and trees grow on the Earth.

The creation story

When God first created the universe, the Earth was dark and covered in water.

On the first day God made light and separated it from the darkness. He called the light 'day and the darkness 'night'.

On the fourth day God made the sun, moon and stars to light up the sky and separate night from day.

On the fifth day God made all the creatures that live on the Earth. He made fish for the sea, birds for the air and animals and insects for the land.

On the sixth day God made human beings. He put them in charge of everything He had created and told them to look after it.

On the seventh day God rested. The universe was complete.

What do Christians believe about the creation story?

Some Christians, called fundamentalists, believe that the universe was created exactly as it says in the creation story. Other Christians, however, think it is a myth. Myths are stories that explain mysterious events, unusual traditions or strange sights in nature. Myths have usually been passed on by word of mouth for hundreds of years before being written down.

Scientists have challenged the belief of some Christians about creation. They say that it took much longer than six days for the universe to be formed and believe in the theory of **evolution**. Many other Christians agree with them.

Some astronomers believe that about eighteen billion years ago a huge explosion created the universe. This is called the 'Big Bang' theory. Some Christians say this may be one way to prove that God created the universe out of nothing.

How were humans created?

Charles Darwin (1809–1882 CE) was a Church of England minister, but he was also a scientist. He went on a scientific study trip to South America on the ship HMS *Beagle*. The trip lasted five years and, during this time, Darwin developed what is called the 'theory of evolution'.

- Darwin believed that humans were not created by God but that they 'evolved', or developed, from more primitive creatures. He wrote a book called *The Origins of the Species*, which caused great discussion and made some people question whether the creation story in the Bible is true.

The environment

In this section you will:
- find out about why Christians believe they should look after the environment and learn about some of the ways they care for it
- be able to recognize some of the environmental problems which concern people
- learn about some important Christian charities working to help the poor and the environment.

Why do Christians believe they should care for the environment?

Christians believe that the Earth and everything in it belongs to God. They believe that God put human beings in charge of the Earth and gave them the job of looking after it. This is called **stewardship**. Christians also believe that God will judge them on the way they have looked after or treated His creation.

Another reason why Christians look after the environment is because they know that it provides what they need to live. In the autumn, Christians have a harvest festival. This is when they say a special thank you to God for all His goodness and praise him for the beauty and fruitfulness of nature. Christians take gifts of fruit, flowers and vegetables to decorate the **church** for this festival. After the service everything is given away to people in need who live nearby.

How do Christians care for the environment?

Christians try to look after the environment in all sorts of ways. Individuals and groups may recycle rubbish, and try to keep areas litter free. They may try to buy products which are packaged in biodegradable materials. Christian groups have also set up national and international organizations, which protect the environment.

The Christian Ecology Link (CEL) publishes a magazine called *Green Christians*, and reminds Christians of their responsibility to care for the environment. CEL organizes events such as National Car-free Day, Walk to School Weeks and Cycling Festivals. These events remind the public of the damage cars can do to people's health and the environment.

Another organization, the European Christian Environmental Network (ECEN), encourages Christians in 26 countries to take part in a wide range of environmental projects. The issues they deal with include the effects of climate change and genetic engineering.

The work of Christian charities such as Christian Aid, Tearfund and CAFOD (Catholic Aid for Overseas Development)

Christian Ecology Link (CEL) symbol

European Christian Environmental Network (ECEN) symbol

Christian aid agencies try to set up self-sustainable programmes of development. Here, CAFOD is distributing buckets in Albania

shows how people in poor countries are affected when we don't care for the environment. They also work hard to make sure that the Earth's resources are shared out more fairly.

Christian Aid

Christian Aid is a charity which is supported by many different Christian **denominations**. Christian Aid works to try to put an end to poverty and child labour. The charity provides educational materials for schools, and gives practical support for developing countries. Christian Aid is trying to change international trade laws which allow rich countries to pay very low wages to workers in poor countries to make products which are then sold at a high cost. The charity campaigns to stop children being treated as slaves.

Tearfund

Tearfund is a Christian charity which aims to help and bring hope to communities around the world. The charity also tells the people they help about Jesus and Christianity. Tearfund is involved in a number of different projects, including Tearcraft. Tearcraft sells a variety of fairly traded products, such as coffee, in the United Kingdom and Ireland.

Moral issues 1

In this section you will:
- learn how Christians decide what is right and what is wrong
- find out what Christians think about animal rights
- think about animal cloning.

What is a moral issue?

A **moral** issue is something that could be considered to be right or wrong. Some people might say it is right and others may say it is wrong. Different people will have different ideas about what is right and what is wrong. This may be for religious reasons or because people have different values or traditions.

The word **immoral** means 'wrong'. When someone behaves immorally their behaviour is not acceptable when judged by the agreed standards and rules.

The word **amoral** means 'without moral standards'. Someone who is amoral shows no understanding of right and wrong.

How do Christians decide what is right and what is wrong?

Christians make decisions about what is right and what is wrong by thinking about how God wants them to live their lives. They ask, 'What would Jesus do in this situation?' and try to follow his example. They can find out what Jesus might have done by reading the **Gospels** in the **New Testament**. They also try to follow the Ten Commandments, which are written in the **Old Testament**. Using the Bible to help with moral issues can be difficult for Christians. The writers did not have to face many of the problems of the modern world and Jesus lived in a time which was very different from today. Christians need to think things through for themselves and make their own decisions according to their conscience. Sometimes they may ask **Church** leaders or other Christians for advice before deciding what to do.

Animal rights

Christians believe that animals are an important part of God's creation, but they may have different views about how they should be treated. Most Christians do not believe that animals have the same rights as human beings, but that they should still be treated with kindness and respect. Many Christians disagree with animals being used to test make-up or toiletries, such as shampoo, but some accept using animals to test medicines to cure humans or other animals. Many Christians disagree with intensive farming such as keeping chickens in small cages and 'blood sports' such as hunting.

Other groups of Christians believe that humans should not do to animals what they would not do to themselves. The Religious Society of Friends, known as Quakers, has always been very concerned about the rights of animals. Many of them

An animal rights protest against Spanish monkey farms

welfare. Sometimes they organize church services where worshippers pray for sick and suffering animals. Some Churches allow animals to go to these services. This idea comes from a verse in the Bible which says that all of God's creation should come together to worship God (Ephesians 1: 10).

are vegetarians and do not wear fur or go to circuses with animals, or visit zoos.

Christians founded the Royal Society for the Prevention of Cruelty to Animals (RSPCA), and there are other Christian organizations that care for animals. Animal Christian Concern (ACC) was set up by May Tripp who noticed that her dog had its own personality. One day, when her dog was ill and in pain, May began thinking about all the other animals that suffer at the hands of humans and she decided to do something to protect them. The ACC encourages Christians and non-Christians to work together for animal

Animal lives for human lives?

Many Christians are very concerned about recent scientific experiments with animals, which attempt to clone exact copies of another animal. 'Dolly' the sheep was the first successful animal clone, cloned at the Roslin Institute in Edinburgh in 1996.

In 2001, piglets were cloned to provide organs, such as hearts and kidneys, which could be used to replace diseased organs in human beings. This has made many people question whether it is morally right to use animals in this way. Some people say that cloning is no different to raising pigs to provide bacon or pork for food. Others say that using animal organs in humans could pass on animal diseases to them. The debate leaves Christians with a moral dilemma: Is it right, in the eyes of God, to do to animals what we would not do to humans?

Moral issues 2

In this section you will:

● find out how Christians believe we should treat each other

● learn about what Christians think about prejudice and discrimination

● read about Oskar Schindler.

Christian attitudes towards prejudice and discrimination

Prejudice is when you make up your mind about someone without knowing what he or she is really like. **Discrimination** is when you behave in a certain way because of what you think you know about someone or a group of people. If you discriminate against a person or a group, you treat them worse than other people.

There are many different kinds of prejudice, and discrimination can take many forms. People are discriminated against for all sorts of reasons, such as their size or shape, the way they speak, their race or the colour of their skin, disability or age. Discrimination on the basis of race or skin colour is called racism. Treating everyone the same is called equality.

Prejudice leads to stereotyping. This is when you judge a group of people to be the same and expect everyone in the group to behave in the same way.

Christians believe that everyone is created and loved by God and should be treated equally. The Bible tells us that Jesus did not discriminate against anyone. He told his followers to follow the golden rule: treat everyone as you would like to be treated. Jesus taught that you cannot love God and not love your neighbour. He told a story, called a **parable**, about the Good Samaritan to teach his followers that 'neighbour' means anyone who is in need. This kind of Christian love is called **agape**. Agape means that you help and care for others without expecting anything back.

'… God treats everyone on the same basis.'

(Acts 10: 34)

'… From one human being [God] created all races on earth and made them live throughout the whole earth.'

(Acts 17: 26)

'… there is no difference between Jews and Gentiles, between slaves and free men, between men and women; you are all one in union with Christ Jesus.'

(Galatians 3: 28)

How have Christians responded to prejudice and discrimination?

Dr Martin Luther King

Dr Martin Luther King was a Black American civil rights leader and Baptist minister. He used non-violent protests to fight for equality for black people and white people in the southern states of the USA.

'… I have a dream that my four little children will one day… not be judged by the colour of their skin but by the content of their character…'

Dr Martin Luther King

Nelson Mandela

Nelson Mandela, a black South African leader, was in prison for 28 years. He fought to end **apartheid** which kept black and white people apart.

'… Let there be justice for all. Let there be peace for all. Let there be work, bread, water and salt for all…'

Nelson Mandela

Many Christians believe that Mother Teresa was a good example of agape love

Mother Teresa

Mother Teresa, a Roman Catholic nun, spent her life in India, helping people who were homeless and dying, without thinking about which religion or race they belonged to. She saw everyone as equal in the eyes of God.

'There is only one God and He is God to all…'

Mother Teresa

'Schindler's List'

Oskar Schindler was a factory owner in Czechoslovakia. At the start of the Second World War, he used Jewish slave labourers in his factories. Schindler could treat them as he liked, and could pay them nothing, because eventually many of them would be sent to Nazi concentration camps, where they would probably be killed. Schindler became very rich but, after a while, he began to see how terribly wrong the Nazi treatment of the Jews was. He came to believe that the Jews needed help.

Schindler began to do everything he could to save as many Jews as possible, often at great risk to himself. Many Jews owed their lives to him. At the end of a film called 'Schindler's List', Schindler is presented with a ring by his assistant, who is a Jew called Itzhak Stern. Inside the ring are the words, 'Whoever saves a life, saves the world entire.'

Ultimate questions 1

In this section you will:

- find out what people mean by ultimate questions
- think about how believing that God exists can explain some of life's mysteries
- read and reflect upon a poem about life after death.

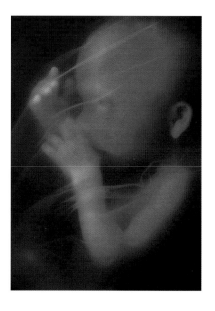

What is an ultimate question?

There are many things in life that puzzle us and cannot easily be explained. For example, 'Is there really a God?' or 'How did life begin?' These are ultimate questions. People ask ultimate questions to try to make sense of the world in which they live or to try to find out what is the purpose of their own life. The way in which people try to answer ultimate questions depends on their beliefs. Christianity, like other religions, has beliefs which try to give answers to ultimate questions, or at least to give people hope that there may be answers to them.

Christians believe that all life is a precious gift from God. They believe that we exist because God chooses to give us life. He made us all unique and special and loves each and everyone of us. The idea that life is sacred because it comes from God is called **sanctity of life**. Because Christians believe in the sanctity of life many find it hard to accept abortion and euthanasia.

Why do we exist?

'Then God said, "And now we will make human beings; they will be like us and resemble us…" So God created human beings, making them to be like himself. He created them male and female…'

Genesis 1: 26–7

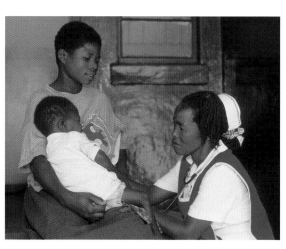

'My commandment is this: love one another as I have loved you.' (John 15: 12)

What are we here for?

Christians believe that God created human beings for a reason, and that life on Earth is part of God's plan for us. They believe that our relationship with God begins in this life on Earth and goes on after we die. Christians say that the reason they are here is so they can love and serve God. They believe that humans are made 'in the image of God' and when they care for other people they are showing their love for God and doing what God would do.

'The dying, … the unwanted, the unloved – they are all Jesus in disguise.'

Mother Teresa

What happens when we die?

Christians believe in everlasting life. They think that when someone dies, the soul, that is a person's spirit, lives on. Christians believe that God gives life and gives

people the chance to live with Him when they die. God judges and decides whether someone has lived a good enough life to be with Him in a state called Heaven. If someone has lived a bad life, they believe they will be separated from God in a state called Hell. Some Christians think that not many people can hope to go straight to Heaven, and Roman Catholics believe that most people go through a stage of preparation called **purgatory**.

'All is Well'

The following is part of a poem often read at Christian funerals. Christians believe they will meet their loved ones again when they die.

'Death is nothing at all
I have only slipped away into the next room
I am I and you are you
Whatever we were to each other
That we still are…

… Life means all that it ever meant
It is the same as it ever was
There is absolute unbroken continuity…

Why should I be out of mind because I am out of sight?
I am but waiting for you
For an interval
Somewhere very near
Just around the corner
All is well.'

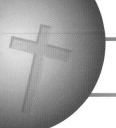

Ultimate questions 2

In this section you will:
- look at how Christians respond to the problems of evil and suffering
- think about the rights and wrongs of euthanasia.

Flooding in the United Kingdom

Why do people suffer?

This is one of the most difficult questions to answer.

Many people say that if God existed and cared about us, He would not let us suffer. Others say that God is not powerful enough to stop all the suffering. Some people think that suffering is a natural part of being a human and that God helps them to cope with it.

Some people's lives change because of what they have suffered. Some turn to God and others lose their faith and turn away from God. Some say they are stronger, better people because of what they have been through.

'My faith died along with my daughter. I gave her a Christian burial because everyone expected me to but as I stood at her graveside, I thought this is pointless. There is no God.'

'I was christened as a baby but I never really thought about God at all until I became ill with cancer. One day when I was feeling really depressed and unhappy, a friend of mine, who is a Christian, persuaded me to go to church with her.

I don't really know what happened but I came out of the service feeling a sense of peace and I felt hopeful about my life for the first time in months. I went to church regularly after that and I've recently decided to get confirmed.'

Where does suffering come from?

Sometimes natural disasters such as earthquakes or floods cause terrible suffering. These are called natural disasters because humans do not usually cause them. Suffering as a result of evil acts of violence, terrorism and war is

Earthquake devastation in India

caused by humans. Evil means wrong or wicked. We say that something is evil when it causes harm to people on purpose. Sometimes we cause suffering by accident – it is not something we plan but other people suffer because of our actions.

What is the Christian response to suffering?

The **Christian** writer C.S.Lewis (author of *The Chronicles of Narnia*) once said that 'pain is God's megaphone for rousing a deaf world'. He thought that pain and suffering is God's way of getting people to turn to Him. C.S. Lewis also thought that God is like a sculptor trying to make a perfect statue. He said that pain and suffering is God's chisel, his way of changing us, making us better people.

Most Christians believe that God created human beings with **free will**, which means they can choose to do good or evil. It is because humans choose to do evil that there is pain and suffering in the world.

Some Christians believe there is a supernatural evil force in the world called the Devil which tries to make people do wicked things. They believe that the Devil is responsible for evil in the world.

Other Christians see suffering as a sort of test. This idea comes from the Bible story about a man called Job. It tells how Job was tested through terrible suffering to see if he would still worship and praise God.

Another viewpoint is that you just have to trust that God knows what He is doing. Many Christians believe that if you have suffered on earth you will be rewarded by God in Heaven. Christians are taught that they should praise and worship God, no matter what happens in their lives, because God will give them the strength to cope with it.

Most Christians say that God understands what it is like to suffer and be in pain. They say this is because Jesus suffered and died on the cross.

Euthanasia or hospice?

The word euthanasia means 'easy death'. It refers to when someone is helped to die in order to save them from further suffering and pain. This is a very serious matter, and people have different views about it. Euthanasia is against the law in almost every country, but some people want the law changed.

All Christian **Churches** are against euthanasia. They say that life comes from God and that only God has the right to end it. Christians believe that everything possible should be done to relieve suffering, and the first hospices were set up by Christians. A hospice is where people who are terminally ill (dying) can go to receive care and medicine which will ease their suffering. The hospice staff will also care for and support the family of the sick person.

Glossary

Agape unconditional, self-sacrificing, non-romantic love which Christians believe they should try to demonstrate to others

Amoral without moral qualities, characteristics

Anointed being smeared with consecrated oil

Anointing of the Sick being anointed with holy oil during some ceremonies

Apartheid a system of racial segregation in South Africa

Apocrypha (from a Greek word meaning 'hidden') a collection of seven books which the Roman Catholic Church accepts as part of its scriptures

Apostles (from the Greek word 'to send') the name given to the original twelve disciples of Jesus. Christians believe they were 'sent out' into the world by God to tell people about Jesus

Ascension the belief that Jesus went up (ascended) into the presence of God (Heaven)

Baptism the ceremony by which some people become members of the Christian Church

Baptistry a small pool containing enough water for a person to be fully immersed during a baptism ceremony

Believers' baptism a ceremony by which young people or adults become full members of the Christian Church

Blasphemy being disrespectful to God

Chrismation a ceremony carried out straight after baptism in the Orthodox Church

Christ the name given to Jesus by his followers after his death when they believed he had been resurrected

Christians the name given to the followers of the Christ (Jesus)

Church the name given to the building in which Christians worship; different denominations within Christianity; the worldwide Christian community

Clergy a group of people who are ordained and authorized to lead worship and look after the congregation of a church in a Christian denomination

Confession the act of admitting to God, through a priest, what one has done wrong and expressing sorrow and regret for it

Confirmation the ceremony where Christians publicly confirm the vows made on their behalf at baptism and become full or grown up members of the Christian Church

Congregation a group of people who have gathered together for worship

Consecrated holy, blessed, set apart; something which is made holy and set aside for religious purposes

Creed (from the Latin word *credo* meaning 'I believe') a statement of belief

Crematorium a building in which corpses are cremated

Cross the symbol of Christianity

Crucifix a particular kind of cross which has an image of Jesus on it

Denomination a separate Christian group which shares the same name and beliefs

Disciples followers of Jesus including the twelve men Jesus chose especially to help him carry out his work on earth

Discrimination the action taken as a result of prejudice

Divine godlike

Easter Day the day Christians celebrate their belief in Jesus' resurrection, one of the most joyful and happy days in the Christian year

Ecumenical belonging to the 'world-wide' Christian Church

Episcopal (from the Greek word meaning 'bishop') a term used to describe a Church which has bishops

Epistles long and usually quite formal letters containing Christian teachings

Eternal life the belief that life continues after death

Eucharist the name given to a service of Holy Communion; it means 'thanksgiving'

Evolution the gradual and natural development of the universe over a long period of time

Forgiveness to forgive or be forgiven, to stop thinking badly of someone or for wrong actions to no longer be counted against a person

Free will the idea that God has given human beings the freedom to choose how to behave

Genuflection a series of movements made during worship to show respect for God

Good Friday the day on which Christians remember Jesus' death

Gospels (from a Greek word meaning 'good news') the first four books of the New Testament: Matthew, Mark, Luke and John. These tell the story of Jesus and his teachings.

Great Schism the split of the Christian Church into two parts, the Catholic Church and the Orthodox Church, in 1054

Hebrew the language of the Jewish people

Heresy a belief which is different to the official teachings of the Christian Church

Holy associated with God, sacred

Holy Communion a church service during which Christians share bread and wine together in memory of Jesus; the act of receiving bread and wine during the Eucharist

Holy Saturday the last day of Lent, the day before Easter Day, when Christians get ready to celebrate their belief in Jesus' resurrection

Holy Spirit the third person of the Trinity, an invisible divine power which guides and inspires human beings

Holy water water which has been blessed and put aside for holy purposes such as baptism

Holy Week the period in the Christian year when Christians focus on the events associated with the death and resurrection of Jesus

Humility being humble, showing that you recognize your failings and weaknesses

Immoral unacceptable, wrong behaviour

Incarnation the act of God becoming a human being in Jesus

Incense a sweet-smelling substance which gives off an odour when burnt

Infant baptism a ceremony by which children are welcomed into the Christian Church

Interfaith involving different religions

Laity ordinary members of a Christian congregation who have not been ordained

Last Supper the name given to the final meal Jesus shared with his disciples

Lectionary a book containing an ordered set of Bible readings for Christians to study at set times throughout the year

Liturgy (from a Greek word meaning 'service') the set form of service used by a church

Marriage the religious or legal ceremony by which people become husband and wife

Martyrs people who suffer or die for their beliefs

Maundy Thursday the day before Good Friday when Christians remember the final meal or Last Supper Jesus had with his disciples

Meditation a form of quiet prayer which involves clearing the mind of all distractions and concentrating on God

Messiah (**Mashiah**) Hebrew word meaning the 'Anointed One', a saviour sent from God

Midnight Mass special service held late at night on Christmas Eve to commemorate the birth of Jesus

Ministry time spent in the service of God

Missionaries people who are sent to other places by their church to spread the Christian faith.

Moral conforming to accepted good standards of general behaviour

New Testament a collection of Christian writings which include the Gospels

Old Testament the Christian name for the Jewish scriptures, the first part of the Christian Bible

Ordination the service by which a person becomes a priest

Pacifists people who disagree with the use of violence

Palm Sunday the day Christians commemorate Jesus arriving in Jerusalem on a donkey shortly before he was crucified. It is the last Sunday of Lent and the first day of Holy Week

Parable a short story which makes a religious or moral point

Paschal candle a large candle which is lit in many churches on Holy Saturday to represent the light of Jesus

Penance a voluntary act to make up or atone for wrongdoings

Pilgrim the name given to someone who goes on a religious journey or pilgrimage

Pilgrimage a religious journey

Pope the leader of the Roman Catholic Church

Prayer a way of approaching or communicating with God

Prejudice to prejudge someone for no good reason

Priest the title given to people who have been ordained and are authorized to lead worship and look after the congregation in the Anglican, Roman Catholic and Orthodox Churches. Priests are also known as vicars in the Church of England

Prophets important people in the Bible who are believed to have been inspired by God

Protestant (from the word 'protest') the name given to the new Churches which were formed as a result of the Reformation

Psalms a collection of 150 religious songs, poems and prayers which are sung or chanted during Christian services or ceremonies

Purgatory according to Roman Catholic belief, a state after death where the soul is purified and made ready to go to Heaven

Reconciliation the idea that Jesus' death repaired the relationship between God and human beings and brought them together

Redeemer a title Christians have given to Jesus because they believe he rescued or freed people from the consequences of their sins

Redemption the idea of Jesus saving human beings from the consequences of their sins

Reformation a religious revolution in the Catholic Church during the sixteenth century

Repentance showing regret for wrongdoings, turning away from sin and living the way God wants

Resurrection the belief that Jesus rose from the dead and overcame death

Revelation God revealing or making Himself/Herself known to human beings

Rites of passage rituals which mark important human experiences such as baptism, confirmation, marriage and death

Sacrament a sacred experience or event where Christians believe they receive special blessings from God

Saint someone who has been recognized after their death as being especially holy and dedicated to God whilst they were alive

Salvation Army a Protestant denomination founded by William Booth in 1865, which is organized in a military way and has its own uniform

Sanctity of life the idea that all life is precious and sacred because it is a gift from God

Saviour a person who has saved someone. This is a title Christians have given Jesus because they believe he saved people from the consequences of their sins

Scriptures writings inspired by God

Second Coming the belief that Jesus will return to Earth one day to finally judge human beings

Secular non-religious

Sermon the part of the service when the priest talks to the congregation about some aspect of Christian belief and practice

Shrine a special area associated with a holy person or object

Sins thoughts or actions that go against the will of God

Stewardship the idea that human beings have a responsibility to look after the earth

Tenakh Jewish name for the Old Testament

Trinity the belief that there are three persons within the one God: the Father, the Son and the Holy Spirit

Vestments special clothing worn by members of the clergy when they take part in worship

Virgin Mary a title given to Mary the mother of Jesus which reflects the Christian belief that she was a pure and good person

Index